Simply
Clematis

Clematis Made Simple

Simply
Clematis

Clematis Made Simple

by Edith M. Malek
photographs by the author

Published by the American Clematis Society
P. O. Box 17085
Irvine, CA 92623-7085

ISBN 0-9670538-1-1

First Printing 2004

Images scanned by LTL Imagery, USA
Line drawings scanned by MicroAdvantage, Inc., USA
Printed & bound by Star Standard Industries, Singapore

Photographs: page 1 *C.* 'Rouge Cardinal' & *C.* 'Belle of Woking',
page 2 *C.* 'Prince Charles' & *C. viticella* 'Alba Luxurians',
page 3 *C.* 'Barbara Jackman' & *C.* 'Piilu'.

To my husband Ken, the love of my life and the wind
beneath my wings.

C. 'Marie Boisselot'

ACKNOWLEDGEMENTS

My thanks to all the wonderful members of
the American Clematis Society for their unwavering belief and
support. They are the driving force behind me striving to make
our society not only informative but fun.

A special note of appreciation to Marsha Stout, who graciously
provided me with the user-friendly pronunciations of the clematis
names in this book.

And last, but not least, to my loving family and friends, thank you
for your patience, understanding and encouragement in the pursuit
of my clematis dreams.

C. 'Jackmanii' with a white bougainvillea and *Antigonon leptopus.*
Opposite: C. 'Belle of Woking'

CONTENTS

INTRODUCTION

Dear Clematis Enthusiast,

    This is my second book about clematis and, just like the first, it is devoted exclusively to growing clematis in the United States. The purpose of this book is to show American gardeners a simple way to grow clematis. I am not afraid to try new ideas and do not blindly accept the traditional doctrines of my predecessors. I have questioned the myths that surround clematis and because of this I believe I have opened the door affording a much greater number of gardeners the opportunity to experience the joy of growing clematis.

    In 1994 I started my odyssey with clematis and have never looked back. Being a clematis pioneer has taken a certain amount of courage because of some of the setbacks I have encountered, but I feel the journey has been well worth it. I hope you will join me in helping to realize my life's ambition of making this beautiful and versatile plant as "Recognizable as the Rose" in America.

C. 'Ville de Lyon' with *Rosa* 'Gertrude Jekyll'.

Clematis forever!

Edith M. Malek
(a.k.a. the "Clematis Queen")

My arch in Irvine, CA adorned with *C.* 'Star of India', *C.* Mdm. Baron
Veillard, *C.* 'Ville de Lyon' and *Rosa* 'Gertrude Jekyll'.

9

The Future for Clematis in the United States

My vision for clematis in America is to give gardeners a clear understanding of where clematis can grow here. This can be accomplished through research and documentation and even experimentation. It is all right to take chances and not just follow the flock. Be a pioneer.

I hope this book inspires you to start or expand your clematis collection. There is nothing wrong with the venerable standbys that are currently being offered to us and many should be included in your garden, but the clematis featured in this book are only the tip of the iceberg. The possibilities are infinite. We need to encourage American nurseries to carry more of these fabulous vines.

With continued exposure the popularity of clematis will increase. With increased popularity there comes more demand. With more demand there comes more selection. With more selection there comes more recognition.

I believe by changing attitudes and proper education, more American gardeners will come to enjoy the pleasures of clematis. Considering what those pleasures bring, the future looks bright!

C. texensis 'Duchess of Albany' with climbing *Rosa* 'Winifred Coulter'.

The vision must be followed by the venture.
It is not enough to stare up the steps - We must step up the stairs.
— *Vance Havner*

C. 'Multi Blue'

C. 'Margaret Hunt', *C.* 'Star of India', *C. viticella* 'Minuet' and *C. viticella* 'Royal Velours'.

11

OLD WIVES TALES
SETTING THE RECORD STRAIGHT

Until recently, with a few exceptions, gardeners in this country have not had the pleasure of enjoying this exquisite flower to the same degree that our friends overseas have. The reason for this lack of exposure can be attributed to the many myths that have unfortunately surrounded this beautiful plant. Happily, this situation is changing as magazines and newspapers all over the country begin to feature articles describing clematis in glowing terms.

Despite what you may have heard or read about clematis being difficult to grow, nothing could be further from the truth. Clematis have earned this reputation for being difficult because of the numerous "urban legends" that have attached themselves to this clinging vine.

Probably the grandmother of all of these "old wives tales" is "Plant their heads in the sun and their feet in the shade." This widely accepted belief that clematis need a cool root run preserves the myth that clematis are not heat tolerant. Clematis grow equally well when their roots are in full sunlight or in shade. Shading clematis with other plants that have aggressive roots can actually stunt the clematis's growth because these plants can inhibit the clematis from absorbing water and nutrients.

The assumption that clematis are not heat tolerant has led people to believe that clematis cannot grow in relatively hot locations. It is true, no doubt, that clematis will not grow in areas such as Death Valley, but this does not preclude them from being grown in many other hot locales in the United States. For these especially hot locales I would suggest growing the many different small hybrid viticellas or certain large hybrids: 'Victoria', 'Star of India' and 'Ernest Markham' are ones to consider. My advice is to plant clematis with companion plants that are compatible with clematis in filtered shade to help protect them from excessive heat.

Several of the myths have come about from utilizing information in books written for European gardeners. An example would be the myth that clematis are alkaline lovers. The reason this opinion was so readily accepted was that clematis were found growing in the wild in soil with concentrations of chalk and limestone. Since both these compounds are highly alkaline it was assumed that clematis preferred to be in an alkaline planting location. However, with England's ever-present rainfall helping to leach away the lime and chalk present in the soil, several British clematarians are now beginning to question the value of adding lime to the planting site.

I am opposed to adding lime to the soil because it increases the alkalinity of the soil, which can be harmful to clematis. In some areas of the U.S. where there is not a lot of rainfall the soil may be highly alkaline. In these areas it is a good gardening practice to add gypsum or gypsite to your garden in the spring and again in the fall, especially if your soil has tested above 7.0. These products will help to reduce the pH of your soil.

The only exception to the rule of not adding lime would be if you live in an area that has a *major* calcium deficiency. Have your soil tested by a professional soil lab and add lime only if their findings recommend that you do so.

I have found that in this country it is better to grow clematis in the more acidic planting situation of a pH of 6.5. Growing clematis in an acidic location is important for gardeners who live in areas where there is little rainfall. This is especially true for gardeners who already have a high concentration of lime in their soil. Adding gypsum or gypsite reduces the pH wherever high alkalinity is a problem.

GROWING ZONES
WHO'S RIGHT?

Until recently, most of the information available to us about growing clematis has been in books from Great Britain. The problem with relying on the wisdom of the British authors when it comes to growing zones is that their experience is based solely on zones that are similar to our USDA Hardiness Zones 8 and 9. This is because these are the two zones that most closely parallel the growing zones that are prevalent in England.

With our 11 very unique climate zones, this limits the scope of understanding that our British friends have concerning how clematis grow here. Great Britain does not encounter the same light conditions we do. We are located closer to the equator and can have as much as ten times more light intensity. In many parts of this country we can experience much less precipitation and higher temperatures, or harder

C. 'Victoria' with a yellow climbing rose.

C. 'Niobe'

frosts and longer winters. All these environmental conditions can have a major effect on how, when and where clematis will bloom here.

Since there have never been any comprehensive studies conducted in the U. S. that definitively specify where clematis will successfully grow here, the question is "How were these growing zones originally assigned to each specific clematis?". In order to have a complete understanding of how clematis cultivars, and especially species, perform in this country, we need scientific documentation.

Verifying correct growing zones is one of the American Clematis Society's goals and we hope to achieve it by obtaining grant funding. Another way our society is trying to confirm where clematis will grow is by providing our members with yearly blooming charts. What you can do as a clematis enthusiast is to let your mail order and retail sources for clematis know when a plant does in fact grow in a zone not ascribed to it. Admittedly, there needs to be much more done in this area, but at least it can help us to more fully understand what it takes to grow this alluring flowering vine.

CLIMATE ZONES

I am a great proponent of both the *Official USDA Plant Hardiness Zone Map* that was most recently revised in 1990 and the *Sunset National Garden Book* zones because I feel their maps are an invaluable tool for gardeners. I find the revised USDA map particularly useful because of its inclusion of the intra-zones "a" and "b". For the purpose of this book, when referring to zones, the 1990 *Official USDA Plant Hardiness Zone Map* will be used.

Those of us who garden in the West have been most fortunate to have available to us the *Sunset Western Garden Book* (a gardener's bible), which divides eleven of our Western states into 24 zones. Additionally, in 1997 *Sunset* magazine introduced a system for the whole country that now utilizes 45 climate zones in their *Sunset National Garden Book*.

Although I have included the *Official USDA Plant Hardiness Zone Map* in this book, for those of you who are interested in a more precise look at and understanding of climate zones, I highly recommend you purchase the *Sunset National Garden Book*. It is also an excellent reference tool for making decisions about where to plant over 6,000 plants in the 45 climate zones they have designated. The only

15

reservation I have is that I disagree with their assessments of where clematis will prosper. I am hoping that we will be able to change their current evaluation with the information our society receives from our members annually submitting their clematis blooming period forms.

At the time this book, *Simply Clematis,* was published a new USDA Plant Hardiness Zone Map had been introduced by *The American Horticultural Society.* This new map consists of 15 zones instead of the 11 zones used on the 1990 map but it has yet to be officially implemented.

Since only *minimum* temperatures are taken into account on the official USDA Map, it should only be used as a guideline. Because the zone maps do not show heat, humidity or other factors that could affect your plant, many microclimates may exist within a zone. It may be possible, for example, for Zone 4 conditions to exist within Zone 3.

I believe that USDA Zones 4 through 11 are the most favorable areas for growing clematis. Clematis are cold-hardy vines that can tolerate minimum temperatures below 30°F. They have a high level of success in Zones 4 through 9, which are traditionally cold-winter areas. However, contrary to popular belief, they can also thrive in the warmer-winter temperatures associated with Zones 10 and 11.

Regardless of which map you choose to reference, keep in mind that your plant could care less to which zone it has been assigned. The important thing, as I mentioned before, is that you realize that these maps should only be used as a guideline and had I relied solely on zonal maps I would have never attempted to grow clematis in the first place.

THE POSSIBILITY OF GROWING CLEMATIS IN USDA ZONE 3

Nothing would make me happier than to add one more USDA zone to the list of zones where clematis will grow in this country. I have heard from gardeners in Zone 3 that proudly proclaim that they do grow clematis. I would have liked to have added USDA growing Zone 3 to the profiles in this book but I believe until there is more documentation I must resist the temptation to do so. On the other hand, had I not experimented with growing clematis in one of the "forbidden zones", you would not be reading this book right now.

So, with deference to those of you who live in Zone 3 and experience harsh winter conditions, the following are some clematis to consider and some to avoid.

WINTER HARDY CLEMATIS *Clematis alpina* cultivars *Clematis viticella* cultivars *Clematis integrifolia* cultivars *Clematis* x *durandii* *Clematis macropetala:* 'Blue Bird' 'Maidwell Hall' 'Rosy O'Grady' 'White Swan' Large flowering clematis that require hard pruning. Large flowering clematis from colder parts of the world such as those in the Kivistic collection in Estonia.	**Other Possibilities:** *Clematis vitalba* *Clematis orientalis* *Clematis recta* *Clematis serratifolia* *Clematis tangutica* cultivars 'Elsa Späth' 'Henryi' 'The President' **CLEMATIS TO AVOID:** *Clematis montana* cultivars and *chrysocoma* cultivars as well as any doubles which bloom double in the spring and single later in the season.

CLEARING UP THE CONFUSION

Wouldn't it be wonderful to know exactly when and where a clematis will bloom and how tall it will grow? Unlike other authors, I understand that the specifics when growing clematis in the U.S. can vary dramatically from one USDA Zone to another. There are many variables in this country that influence how clematis do grow. Because of these variables, the blooming periods, color, color intensity, flower size and height range cannot always be specifically pinned down. For this reason, the information I am providing contains no absolutes, but it does give you an educated point of reference. In order to help clear up some of the confusion, here are some of the factors that might impact your clematis.

BLOOMING PERIOD

Blooming times can be influenced by the age of your plant, the location in which you have planted it, how often you feed and water it, which cultivar you have selected and in which USDA zone you live. Clematis, like people, can have good years and bad years. Some clematis will give you all they have one year and then just seem to sulk the following year. Some take a few years to become established before they bloom satisfactorily while others take off immediately. Blooming periods can also be determined by the length of your growing season. The longer the season the more potential there is for repeat performances.

Color and Color Intensity

The coloring of the flowers on your clematis can change from one season to the next or even from day to day. Factors such as how long a flower has been in bloom, the time of the year, weather and exposure to sunlight can affect the intensity of the colors of your flowers. Even from zone to zone this variation of coloring can be experienced by the same variety of clematis. Repeat crops can also exhibit this color variation.

Flower Size & Height Range

Just as with color, many factors can affect the flower size and height range of your clematis. How old your plant is, the planting site you choose, how much light your plant receives, which cultivar you have selected, soil conditions, if your plant is root bound and in which USDA zone you live can all play a significant role in flower size and height range.

Why Clematis Double

I adore double clematis! I know there are some clematis gardeners who are purists and do not find their attributes attractive, but it was love at first sight when I saw pictures of 'Vyvyan Pennell' and 'Veronica's Choice'.

I am not sure why clematis double other than the fact that it is just in their nature to do so. I do, though, have an idea why certain double clematis do not double in certain areas.

When I first started growing clematis the only double cultivar in my collection was *Clematis* 'Proteus'. When I first acquired 'Proteus' I couldn't wait until spring when I was sure it would produce flowers that would have up to 100 frilly tepals. To my disappointment it did not produce those double flowers. I tried to find information about what clematis needed to produce double flowers. The only information I could gather is that you must have old wood to get double flowers.

How old is "old"? Is the answer two to three years old? Since my *Clematis* 'Proteus' was now three going on four years old and was still only producing single flowers, I decided I just had to be patient for my "old" wood to develop. My patience, though, was never rewarded.

Eventually I acquired a 'Vyvyan Pennell' and it produced two of the most beautiful double flowers I had ever seen. I was so excited because I now had a clematis with that elusive "old" wood. I was the proud owner of one of the double clematis I had been longing for. To my great disappointment, the next spring and every subsequent spring, it has only produced crops of single flowers.

I had the mandatory "old" wood now, so why were my flowers not doubling? The answer came to me after importing several other double cultivars from regions colder than Southern California. These imported varieties rewarded me with glorious double blooms in the first spring and, alas, only singles each spring thereafter. I then concluded that clematis which produce doubles only in the spring and then later produce single flowers not only need old wood to do their doubling, they also require a "winter chill".

To my delight I have found that not all doubles need this "winter chill" or "old" wood. Listed in **Appendix E, Double Clematis by Zone**, are doubles that do not require a winter chill or old wood. These clematis would be a welcome addition to gardens in warmer locales that do not experience a winter chill as well as those colder locales where clematis die to the ground due to severe frosts.

So, if you live in a warmer locale or an area that freezes, stick with clematis such as 'Duchess of Edinburgh' or 'Multi Blue' because they consistently produce double flowers in all locales. When new double cultivars are introduced I suggest that you take a wait-and-see approach. *Wait* for more information so you won't *see* your dreams of a double shattered.

C. 'Vyvyan Pennell' ~ single. *C.* 'Vyvyan Pennell' ~ double.

GROWING CLEMATIS
PLANTING

THE BEST TIME TO PLANT. The ideal time to plant clematis is in the spring or fall. In warmer areas of the country, I always suggest waiting for the cooler months before planting. This will help reduce the initial stress to the plant by allowing it to acclimate during a cooler season.

If you have acquired your plant during the summer months and decide to follow my advice and wait until fall to plant, you should leave your clematis in its original nursery container and care for it as if you had planted it in a pot or other container.

THE PLANTING SITE. Having chosen your planting site that is in the correct lighting conditions for your clematis (see page 45), dig a hole a minimum of 18 inches wide by 18 inches deep, preferably 24 inches wide by 24 inches deep. This large hole allows for more room for soil amendment, if needed, and it gives the roots of your clematis room to roam. This major excavation can also improve drainage, another important factor in raising a healthy clematis.

Having dug your hole, the next step in planting should always be preparing the soil. Soil types vary greatly from area to area, but whatever type you are dealing with in your own garden, whether clay, sandy or loam, you will need to add soil amendment before planting your clematis. Do this by mixing the displaced topsoil from the planting hole with soil amendment in the proportions that I recommend below for your soil type.

If you have clay soil or other heavy soil it already has plenty of moisture-holding ability, but the aeration will need to be improved. Do this by making a mixture of 50% high-grade amendment and 50% topsoil.

If you have sandy soil you can improve its moisture-holding ability by adding 30% to 50% high-grade amendment to the topsoil mixture.

If you have loam soil, you have been blessed with the best of all soil types. Even so, adding 20% amendment to your soil would be beneficial.

Once you have prepared your soil, make sure you cut the can and *carefully* remove the rootball. **Never** pull your plant out of the container. If the plant appears rootbound, loosen the outermost roots to encourage proper root distribution.

Add a sufficient amount of your amended topsoil to the hole so that when you position your clematis it will be three inches to five inches below ground level. After placing the clematis in the hole, keep adding the amended soil gently tamping it in until the hole is full. Should your clematis ever get stem rot or suffer any other surface damage, burying it deep gives it a second chance to sprout new stems.

Leave the original support stake or trellis in place until the clematis has had a chance to acclimate to its new home. At that time, remove the old prop and attach the clematis to its permanent support. Generally this should be done after the first year.

Water the clematis thoroughly after planting. Use seaweed extract to help promote root growth.

TRANSPLANTING. The best time to transplant is in the spring or fall. If you decide to transplant, prepare the new planting site following the procedure I have described earlier. When the new site is ready, dig as deeply and as far away as possible from the stem or stems of the plant you are moving. This will allow you to retrieve as much of the rootball as possible. Be careful not to disturb or kink the stem or stems. As you are lifting the clematis out of the ground, be careful to retain as many of the roots as possible. Keeping the roots intact will reduce the amount of stress being placed on the plant. After you have moved the clematis to its new location, water it thoroughly. Use a solution of seaweed extract to help promote root growth. Always remember there is a bit of a risk when transplanting any type of plant and clematis are no exception.

FEEDING

A well-fed clematis is a happy clematis. As with any plant or animal, proper nutrition is vital to proper growth and health. Regardless of age, a poorly fed clematis can produce a stunted plant with a crop of inferior flowers. A well-fed, healthy plant is more capable of resisting disease and less susceptible to stem rot.

The correct time to start feeding depends on the weather. Generally, the ground temperature should be above 55°F. This is when your plant starts to become active and needs nutrients in order to grow. Because your clematis will start to come out of dormancy sooner, those of you who live in milder winter climate zones will need to start a feeding program sooner than those of you living in colder winter zones. Since weather conditions can vary from year to year, so too can the time this emergence from dormancy occurs.

Spring feeding should begin when newly developing leaf stems are about one to two inches long. In USDA Zones 4 through 9 this usually happens some time in March or April, depending upon when the weather starts to warm up.

In Zones 10 and 11, this can happen in late February through early March. Although according to the calendar it may still be winter in Zones 10 and 11, springtime conditions can already exist, necessitating this pre-spring feeding.

In Zones 4 through 9, the final feeding of the year should take place in early September. A feeding later than that could stimulate new growth which might not get a chance to harden off prior to the first frost. The cold of winter, especially in an area where the ground freezes, can damage this tender new growth. You need to conserve the plant's energy for springtime when the new growth has a chance to mature.

For those of you in Zones 10 and 11 who have clematis that continue to bloom into November, the final feeding should take place some time between the end of September and early October, depending on weather conditions. But if you live in an area of Zones 10 or 11 that experiences occasional frost, your last feeding should be in early September for the same reasons that apply to Zones 4 through 9.

The final application in all zones should be with a fertilizer high in phosphorus. This will help flower development the following season. Do not use a fertilizer which is high in nitrogen. This would stimulate new leaf growth, which is unnecessary at this time of year.

FERTILIZERS

As a rule of thumb, any fertilizer that works for roses can be used on clematis. I personally prefer using fertilizers that contain an organic humus base, beneficial microbes and soil conditioners. This enriches your soil while simultaneously feeding your clematis.

Use a fertilizer that is high in phosphorus for the first feeding of the growing season. Then alternate feedings with an all purpose fertilizer making sure that the final feeding is with the high phosphorus fertilizer.

I am not a proponent of using fertilizers that contain sewage sludge, animal or poultry waste, i.e. manure, or animal fecal matter (composted or not). These by-products contain minimal amounts of nutrients as well as a high salt content which can burn the plant's leaves and may also contain toxic levels of heavy metal.

POINTERS FOR FERTILIZING

♦ Follow the manufactures instructions concerning the rate of application and how often to apply the fertilizer.

♦ Keep the fertilizer away from the stems of your clematis to avoid burning them.

♦ When applying granular fertilizer, be careful not to let the fertilizer touch any of the leaves of the plant. Immediately wash off any excess fertilizer that may land on the foliage. This will prevent burning.

♦ Always water thoroughly after applying fertilizer.

♦ Never feed a *sick plant*. It is not good to stimulate new growth when your plant is ailing. It needs to use its energy to recover.

♦ Do not feed a dormant plant.

♦ **Never** add lime or manure where the rainfall is light or the soils are alkaline. Both lime and manure contain salts that can ultimately burn the clematis plant. Lime also inhibits the plant from utilizing essential nutrients such as iron, manganese and zinc.

♦ If your clematis is planted close to a stucco or cement wall, it will need to have additional minor nutrients like iron, manganese and zinc added to the soil, because as the materials in these types of walls break down they turn into lime.

WATERING

Clematis have a reputation for being heavy drinkers. The fact is they only consume average amounts of water. I would suggest watering clematis as you would roses. A good rule of thumb is to always water thoroughly and deeply during the hot summer months. Avoid planting them in waterlogged locations because they will drown.

The location you choose to plant your clematis is an important factor in ensuring that your plant gets an adequate water supply. If a clematis is planted too close to neighboring shrubs or trees it will be in constant competition for water. Try to stay at least four feet away from these friendly rivals.

Properly watering your clematis, especially in its first year, is essential.

This is the time when the new clematis plant is forming its stems and root structure that will support it throughout its life. An established clematis requires a minimum of one gallon of water a week but would benefit during active growing periods with up to four gallons or more depending on weather conditions and how well your soil drains.

Some areas of this country, especially in the West, have a build-up of concentrated salts that can be harmful to your plant. By deep watering you can periodically leach the soil of these accumulations.

Do not rely on Mother Nature to do your watering for you. Even when it rains clematis still need regular amounts of water. If it rains less than one inch in a seven to ten day period, some supplemental watering may be necessary.

During the fall, start reducing the amount of water you give your clematis. Even then though, there can be exceptions such as unseasonably warm or dry weather.

Winter is the time to stop your regular watering regimen, but even during this period, *never* allow the plant to dry out completely. Resume regular watering when your clematis's leaf buds start to swell out from their nodes.

MULCHING

A two-inch to four-inch thick layer of mulch helps the soil retain moisture. It also limits erosion and helps prevent the soil from compacting.

Mulching discourages weeds because it acts as a barrier, preventing seeds from germinating. It is an ideal environment for earthworms and as it decomposes it helps replenish nutrients in the soil, improving its overall composition.

Mulching should be done every spring and again in the fall. Do not let the mulch touch the plant; keep it at least four inches away from its base to prevent rotting.

SUPPORT

The majority of clematis are clinging vines and perform best when grown up some type of support whether man-made or natural. If you allow your clematis to grow on the ground, it increases the possibility of an attack by enemies such as earwigs and snails.

Clematis can grow happily up just about anything with only your imagination limiting the element you choose. They can hide an unsightly chainlink fence, wind around a mailbox post or a lamppost, climb over an arbor or adorn a pergola. The effect of clematis spilling over an umbrella frame, topping a porch entrance, gracing an obelisk or framing an alcove can be dramatic. Growing clematis up one of the beautiful commercial trellises that are available, as well as building your own structures, are other ideas to consider.

Clematis make great companion plants because they intermingle easily with a whole variety of host plants. They will not harm the host plants that are providing them their natural support. Instead, they add to their beauty. Allowing clematis to sprawl through trees, shrubs, roses, vines and other plants provides your clematis with an added benefit of a perfect microclimate. Another plus is that these host plants can also camouflage the clematis during dormancy when they are not looking their best.

It is also a good idea to combine other vines with clematis when you are growing them on man-made structures. This gives you the best of both worlds: an attractive support structure as well as a protective microclimate.

If you are going to use a tree or a large shrub as a support, make sure that you plant your clematis at least four feet away from the trunk. If you choose a small to medium shrub for support, you should plant the clematis two to three feet away. The reason for planting the clematis a little distance away from the supporting plant is to give it its own water supply and rooting area. This keeps it from having to be in constant competition for water and root space.

To decide which plants to combine with your clematis, use one of the many garden encyclopedias or regional gardening guides to help you pick the plants that are appropriate for your unique growing zone.

WINTERIZING: PROTECTING YOUR CLEMATIS FROM WINTER'S WRATH

Winter conditions can vary from zone to zone. Snow cover, early and late frosts and moisture in the soil can all have an effect on your clematis. Winterizing your clematis may be an option or even a necessity in colder locales where the ground freezes and gets down to 15°F or lower. My suggestions for winter care can be useful in areas with dramatic fluctuations in winter temperatures. If you live in an area that requires you to winterize other plants in your garden then I suggest you do the same for your clematis. However, if you have been successfully growing clematis without winter protection and your plants have withstood the rigors of severe winter temperatures, there is no reason to start now.

First of all, it is important to become acquainted with the many microclimates in your garden. For example, clematis planted near the house, along a wall or near a tree are already afforded some degree of protection, while clematis planted in the open are more likely to be damaged by winter weather.

After the ground freezes, when nighttime temperatures drop to 20° F for several days, mulch the roots of your clematis plants with four to six inches of bark, straw or conifer boughs. It is important to wait until the ground is frozen before mulching. The purpose of winter mulching is to keep the soil at a uniform temperature, reducing the possibility of early growth being injured by frost penetration. This mulching can also minimize the damage done to your clematis due to the soil freezing and thawing.

In the spring, after the danger of hard frost has passed, the winter mulch should be removed gradually to prevent rotting. Reapply an all new one-to-two inch thick layer of spring mulch, keeping it eight inches from the stem.

For areas that dip below 15°F, put any containerized clematis in your garden shed or garage.

C. 'Aotearoa' with *Rosa* 'Lavender Lassie'.

Disease & Pest Control

The most common foes that can attack your clematis are stem rot (a.k.a. wilt), powdery mildew, snails and earwigs. Here are some dependable, non-toxic methods that will aid you in your battle against these enemies.

Stem Rot

By far the biggest complaint and most devastating malady to besiege clematis is stem rot. Stem rot is often referred to as "wilt." I prefer the term stem rot because it does not sound so catastrophic.

You will know stem rot when you see it. It strikes quickly without warning. First, the uppermost shoots start to go limp making the plant look as if it needs water. You may water the plant thinking this will solve the problem. But then the young foliage starts to turn brown. Finally, the whole stem collapses and dies. Stem rot can occur on only one stem or affect the entire plant and can happen very rapidly.

There are many opinions about what causes stem rot, but at this time there are no cures. One theory is that it is caused by a fungal infection. For now, preventative measures are the best solution for this woe. Always make sure you buy the biggest, healthiest plant possible. When planting your clematis, avoid kinking any stems. If your clematis should get stem rot, carefully cut off all of the diseased parts of the vine and then disinfect your clippers by dipping them in a horticultural disinfectant after each cut. When finished, dispose of all the diseased stems in a sealed plastic bag to avoid spreading any potential fungal spores.

Powdery Mildew

Powdery mildew is a fuzzy, grayish-white, powdery substance that coats tender new leaves and stems. It can cause unsightly, deformed flowers and crippled leaves and, in severe cases, reduce flower production. It is a fungus that thrives in shady locations and areas of high humidity.

If you live in an area that is prone to powdery mildew you can minimize the risk by selecting a planting site with good air circulation and optimum light conditions. Spot treat with a ready-to-use product that contains neem oil.

Pests

Snails can devour in one night what has taken the clematis several weeks to produce. They are difficult to eliminate totally, so it best to employ numerous methods in your fight against these nasty mollusks. When using bait, use one that contains iron phosphate because it is non-toxic to pets and wildlife. You can also apply copper strip barriers around the base of each plant. For the brave of heart, consider handpicking them at night. If you are into French cuisine you probably already have another solution in mind.

The Phoenix Phenomenon

One of the most disappointing setbacks you as a clematis gardener can encounter is having your gorgeous clematis plant completely collapse. I liken this experience to the mythological bird that symbolizes immortality, resurrection and life after death, the Phoenix. According to legend, this fabled "firebird" burns in flames and later rises from the ashes renewed. Just as the Phoenix, so too can clematis overcome the adversity of crashing and burning. Clematis are very resilient plants and most clematis that have crashed and burned will rejuvenate themselves. I call this particular clematis characteristic the "Phoenix Phenomenon".

What caused it to happen? Was it clematis stem rot (wilt)? I do not believe so. It is more likely that one of the plant's fragile stems was somehow kinked and an adequate supply of water was unable to travel throughout the plant.

Both stem rot (wilt) and the blockage of stems can have the same deadly result: a crashed clematis. The prescription is the same for both: patience. Even after this apparent demise, clematis tend to send up even stronger stems than before.

Should this malady happen to one of your clematis, treat it as though it were any diseased plant and carefully remove the stems of the stricken plant all the way down to the ground. Make sure you sanitize your clippers after each cut and put the dead clippings immediately into a plastic bag making sure they do not make contact with any other clematis in your garden.

So, when the "Phoenix Phenomenon" occurs, be patient. This rise from the ashes can take from as little as a couple of months to a year or longer. And if you took out your clematis insurance policy (you buried it deep) then your clematis will rise to shine again!

Earwigs are omnivorous insects. They tend to eat anything in their path. The damage they do to clematis can be devastating. They love to bore into unopened flower buds and devour big chunks of the flower's tepals.

The simplest remedy for earwigs is a trap. You can construct your own by using a rolled up piece of moistened newspaper, a paper towel roll or a 12" piece of PVC. Place any of these items at the base of your clematis in the early evening. These tubes make perfect hiding places for these nocturnal critters and after a night of foraging they retreat to these shelters to sleep. In the morning, empty the traps into a bucket of hot soapy water.

To a lesser extent aphids, mealybugs, scale, thrips, whiteflies and spider mites can bother your clematis.

Mother Nature has provided us with many beneficial insects that help us fight the battle against these plant pests. These include parasitic wasps, adult ladybugs and the larvae of ladybugs and lacewings.

Sometimes, however, the pest population is too large to be controlled by these garden-friendly insects. This overpopulation usually occurs in the spring (with the exception of thrips) before the beneficial insects are out helping you. Only then should you spray to help eliminate the problem. Use a solution of either insecticidal soap or summer oil (also called light horticultural oil) to combat them.

Ugly Ducklings and Sleeping Beauties

I am often asked about how to prevent ugly leaves from appearing on clematis plants. The obvious answer is to put your plant on a healthy feeding and watering program. But even if you do everything right, spotty leaves, brown edges, dull looking leaves, crispy brown leaves, yellow leaves, etc., especially during the warmer times of the year, can still appear. I have yet to see this phenomenon addressed scientifically and until there is some research done, especially in the area of which growing zones are correct for clematis in this country, we will have to accept this problem as just another one of this plant's personality traits without knowing the reason why it occurs.

The good news is that this malady does not seem to affect the plant's flowering ability. One thing I have noticed is that some of my species plants sometimes generate these unsightly leaves, so all I can surmise is that it might be some fungal or other pathological problem. My personal solution is to surgically remove the ugly leaves that bother me and just ignore the ones that I can live with.

The bottom line is that I do not grow clematis for their foliage. I am aware of the fact that clematis do go dormant and will be ugly in the winter. I also accept that on occasion I will see a clematis in my garden that has a stem or even an entire plant that has crashed because of some unforeseen disaster, but I don't panic. My advice is that if all you are looking for is green foliage then plant something evergreen. Considering how spectacular the flowers these vines produce are, having to occasionally experience a plant that exhibits ugly leaves or even crashes seems to me to be a small price to pay for the beauty that they bestow upon us.

Beyond the subject of ugliness, how do you know if a clematis has died? Well, unless you are willing to take the drastic measure of excavating your plant and performing an autopsy, it is difficult to determine if your plant still has a pulse.

Before you decide to shovel prune, let me point out to you that clematis are very resilient. To paraphrase Mark Twain, the reports of their death can be greatly exaggerated. Over the years I have had several clematis in my garden that have apparently gone to that great flowerbed in the sky, when much to my delight, they experience a miraculous reincarnation.

These second chances at life have taken anywhere from six months to two years to occur. In this book I refer to this event as the "Phoenix Phenomenon". Throughout the years gardeners from all around this country have shared with me their "Phoenix Phenomenon" success stories. Just as in my garden, these clematis survivors have generally been under five years old. My theory is that it affects only plants that are relatively young. Once a plant has become established, its maturity seems to be an insurance policy against many of the catastrophes that can befall clematis.

Regardless of its age though, *do not* remove a clematis just because it appears to be dead. I usually give my plants three years before making that final decision. Unless the lack of space in your garden is a factor, practice some patience. You may very well have an ugly duckling just waiting for the right moment to awaken from its long beauty sleep.

Growing Clematis In A Container

Don't be intimidated or reluctant to grow clematis just because your gardening area is the size of a postage stamp. Clematis can thrive equally as well in containers as they do in the ground. The nice thing about container gardening is that people who live in apartments, townhouses or condominiums, which usually have small decks, balconies or tiny courtyards, can still enjoy the pleasures of growing clematis.

Container gardening provides benefits that traditional gardening does not offer. Since most containers are portable, you can move them out of sight when the plant is dormant or not looking its best. Containers can provide a temporary home while you are deciding on a permanent site. Containers can also be the solution to the problem of having areas in your garden with poor soil conditions.

Just as with growing clematis in the ground, there a few guidelines to follow. (For a list of potential container candidates see **Appendix J, Clematis for Containers**.)

Although they will survive in smaller containers, give your plants a chance to thrive by using containers that are a minimum of 18 inches wide and 18 inches deep. To deter insects and help prevent the soil from falling through the bottom of your container, cover any holes with pieces of screen prior to adding your soil mix.

Do ***not*** add a layer of gravel, crushed rocks, or charcoal in the base of your container. Contrary to what some people may think, this custom does not improve drainage. In fact, just the opposite is true. A layer of these materials creates an area that lacks the amount of surface tension that potting soil has by hindering the gravitational pull, thus delaying drainage. On the other hand, potting soil's consistent texture allows water to drain more readily by distributing the water evenly. Also, using these materials displaces valuable rooting area. It is much more beneficial to fill that space with potting soil.

Place your plant on a layer of fast-draining soilless potting mix. Make sure that the rootball will be buried 3" to 5" below soil level. Add more mix around the perimeter of the plant and gently tamp it down to eliminate any air pockets. Keep adding mix, allowing enough room for adequate watering at the top of the container. Two to three inches from the rim should do the trick.

To promote air circulation, elevate the container leaving an airspace

C. 'Proteus' in a redwood planter box.

of at least half an inch. This can be achieved by using small blocks of wood, rubber washers or the terra cotta "pot feet" specifically designed for this purpose. Doing this also helps with proper drainage.

Clematis grown in a container need some type of support. A trellis, tripod, obelisk or other type of support can be added at the time of planting in the container. It is always a good idea though to leave the original support on your plant until it has acclimated to its new surroundings. Give it a year until you feel the plant is established before removing the original support and attaching it to the new one.

Repot your clematis every three or four years using all new potting mix. When doing so, gently untangle any rootbound roots. As with most potted plants, their roots systems eventually outgrow their containers so, if necessary, upgrade to a larger container.

Feeding and Watering in a Container

A plant in a container is completely dependent upon you for its survival. Because it requires more frequent watering, the nutrients in the potting soil are leached away. These nutrients must be replaced by a regular feeding program.

Start your feeding program either in late winter or early spring when the leaf buds swell and have grown about one inch long. The final feeding in Zones 4 through 9 should be done in the beginning of September. In the milder climates of Zones 10 and 11, where plants tend to have longer blooming cycles, extend your feeding program through the beginning of October.

Since a plant in a container dries out more rapidly than one in the ground, you need to keep a constant vigil. You cannot rely on natural rainfall to adequately provide your clematis with the water it needs. You should always check the moisture content to insure that it is properly maintained. Do not allow the soil to completely dry out but also make sure you do not waterlog it either. If the soil is still moist, watering may not be necessary.

You also need to realize that plants in combination are plants in competition. The rootspace, water and food all have to be shared. The only plants I recommend accompanying your clematis in a container are shallow-rooted annuals or perennials.

Prune Not Doom

One of the most frequently asked questions concerning growing clematis is about how to prune them. The subject of pruning clematis is one of the things that can make a gardener a little apprehensive about owning one. I can identify with the feeling because I can remember the first time I read about how to prune clematis. I thought it was rather perplexing, confusing and far too complicated. Although in the beginning I started out doing it by the book, I eventually realized that what I was doing did not pertain to **my** clematis.

I believe you should never have to lose sleep over cutting back your clematis. Don't be afraid to prune! Even if you cut away too much, your clematis will recover to bloom another day.

There is an adage about how to prune your clematis if you are not quite sure of its identity: "If it flowers before June do not prune". Okay, this is a cute rhyme and it sounds simple enough, but I consider this to be quite misleading and not entirely accurate, especially if you live in USDA Zones 10 and 11. The times when your clematis will bloom can change from year to year. If you live in a locale that has an extremely short growing season, your blooming time should be more predictable.

Many books and articles delve into the issue of "old" and "new" wood as a means to explain what type of pruning will need to be employed. What is "old" and "new" wood? Old wood is any wood that is more than a year old. New wood is new growth that shoots out of the ground or off existing old wood. First blooms of the season that appear on new stems that are close to old wood are still considered to be on old wood. Clematis flowers always appear on the tips of new stems.

Is it really necessary to know if it is "old" or "new" wood? I believe the only time gardeners need to concern themselves with this matter is if they are growing double clematis such as 'Vyvyan Pennell', 'Walter Pennell', 'Proteus', etc., specifically those doubles that produce double flowers only in the spring and then later produce single flowers. These clematis require "old" wood in order to produce their double blooms. So, you would not want to prune the old wood on doubles because you would eliminate their ability to produce double blooms. Clematis that die to the ground each year due to frost or freezing in the colder areas of this country will not produce double blooms because the old wood is destroyed. With this knowledge in mind, deciding whether you are working with old or new wood has little practical value when it comes to your pruning habits.

THE BASIC CUTS AND WHEN TO MAKE THEM

The current thinking on when you should prune your clematis is divided into three categories and is based on when it blooms. These groups are either designated by the letters A, B or C or numbers 1, 2 or 3. Sometimes the group B is subdivided into an even more bewildering B1 and B2. I would like to suggest you abandon pruning your clematis by letters or numbers. Instead, adopt a more sensible approach which is to simply name the pruning methods "light", "hard" or "optional." Do not be concerned when it blooms but rather when the leaf buds swell and what USDA zone you live in. Unless you live in an area of the country that mirrors the weather in Great Britain knowing when a clematis blooms will not be beneficial here and by renaming these categories you will easily know from the heading what steps need to be taken.

So, when do you prune your clematis? The time to prune is when the leaf buds of the clematis begin to show signs of growth. This usually occurs sometime in February or March in Zones 4 through 9 and as early as November in Zones 10 and 11.

When the leaf buds start growing is determined by the weather and, therefore, can change from year to year. Of course, if you live in a colder locale you do not have to worry about pruning because Mother Nature prunes them for you by freezing them right down to the ground.

C. texensis 'Duchess of Albany'

35

Methods of Pruning

In keeping with the title of this book I have provided you with three simple techniques to prune your clematis: **light pruning, hard pruning** and **optional pruning.**

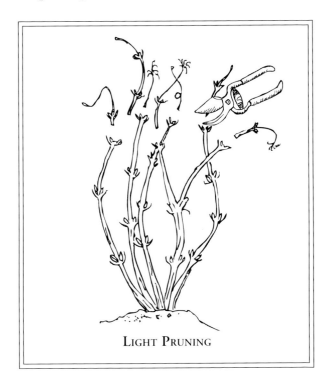

LIGHT PRUNING

Light Pruning

Light pruning is achieved by removing all the dead (see page 41) or damaged wood down to the first pair of healthy leaf buds. Prune off any dead or brown leaves as well as any old petioles that have not attached themselves to something. Leave the healthy stems at their present height. Reposition the stems so that they will form a neat and attractive vine.

Light pruning is the *only* way to prune a double clematis that produces double flowers *only* in the spring and later produces *only* single flowers. If you cut off a stem that produces double flowers you will eliminate its ability to produce doubles the following year, sadly ending up with just a crop of single flowers.

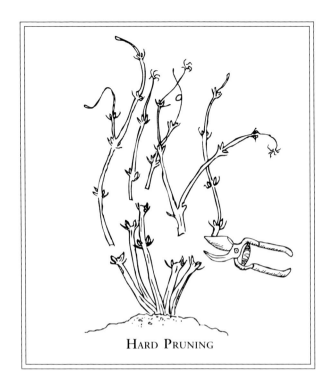

HARD PRUNING

HARD PRUNING

Hard pruning is achieved by cutting back **all** the stems to a length of twelve to eighteen inches. Make your cut just above a pair of healthy leaf buds.

Hard pruning is recommended for clematis varieties that can grow extremely tall. This helps produce a bushier clematis and eliminates containment problems.

OPTIONAL PRUNING

Optional pruning is the best of both worlds because it combines the advantages of both light and hard pruning. It promotes blooms at various heights throughout the vine. It rejuvenates older clematis that have slowed down their flower production. It allows you to plant hard-pruned clematis and light-pruned clematis together. If you are unable to identify which clematis cultivar you have, pruning it by using the optional method is your best bet. This technique leaves some room for error by assuring that should you make a mistake, even with a double clematis, you will not have totally cut off all of the old wood.

Optional pruning is accomplished by combining both light and hard pruning methods on the same plant. By cutting back half or less of the existing stems to a length of twelve to eighteen inches each year, you can acheive this compromise. The remaining stems should be cut back to the first pair of healthy leaf buds.

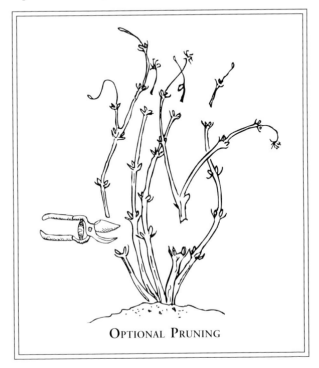

OPTIONAL PRUNING

EARLY TRAINING REQUIRES SOME PRUNING

If you have purchased a clematis that is smaller than a 5-gallon you will need to do some initial training. Small or weak stems should be pruned to a height of twelve to eighteen inches. This is done to reduce the strain on the new clematis's roots by eliminating excess foliage. Stems should be pruned back to a pair of strong, plump leaf buds. I would not recommend pruning stems on clematis plants that have the potential to produce doubles unless the stems are damaged or weak.

If you have bought a 5-gallon plant, which I strongly suggest, early pruning has normally already been done by the wholesaler. Therefore, stems can be either left alone or pruned at your discretion.

To increase flower production in the early stages of your clematis's life, pinch out the tips of the new shoots that are at least twenty-four inches long. This will encourage side branching, resulting in a fuller plant.

Pruning For More Blooms

I live in USDA Zone 10 and have discovered something quite phenomenal about clematis that may possibly hold true in other parts of the U.S. that have extended growing periods. If you hard prune your *texensis*, *viticella* and large hybrid clematis after each blooming period, they can subsequently reward you with another crop of blooms.

I ultimately discovered this phenomenon because my *Clematis* 'Proteus' would get seriously plagued by thrips every summer. I not only hated all of the ugly brown leaves, I was getting sick of spraying it. Finally, I was so fed up, I just whacked it back. Low and behold, in a little over a month and half, I had a new crop of flowers. From then on, by pruning back all the stems each summer, I have obtained three crops of blooms per year instead of the usual two.

I confined this radical pruning technique to my 'Proteus' until I visited one of my favorite wholesale nurseries to purchase some plants, including clematis. The clematis were absolutely beautiful because they were in full bloom. The dilemma, though, was that I could not fit everything into my van. I then decided that it was better to have clematis plants without their flowers rather than not at all, so to get them into my van, I removed their stakes and sacrificed their blooms by cutting them all back to 8". I confess it was a heart wrenching experience leaving behind all my flowers. But, to my surprise, in about six weeks these clematis were blooming again! Since at that point it was too late in the season to experiment, I made a mental note to eventually give this potentially groundbreaking technique a try.

The following year I started experimenting with hundreds of clematis, not only at home but at the nursery where I was working. I employed my new technique and each time the clematis finished their blooming period I would cut them back. Most of the plants would re-bloom, usually within six weeks. This proved to be very valuable for the nursery because the extended blooming season made the plants more saleable since most gardeners prefer to buy their clematis in bloom. It also proved to be valuable to me because of the extended blooming sessions I was able to witness in my garden. This new system allowed the plants to produce three crops per year with even an occasional fourth. Only the weaker cultivars did not respond positively to this pruning technique.

My conclusion is that warm weather is probably a contributing factor to this multi-blooming. Once a plant is pruned all the way back its need for self preservation commands that it produce new growth to survive. The new growth produces new stems which produce new leaves and ultimately flowers. The luxury of being in a warm locale allows the plant the opportunity to repeat this growth and blooming cycle. If you live in a warm locale with enough growing time remaining in the season to produce another crop and you choose to try this technique, I suggest using only strong, vigorous cultivars. Sadly, if a clematis has already proved to be a weak performer, it would probably make a poor candidate for this procedure and nothing you do is going to stimulate it to bloom again.

Important Note: This technique is not meant to replace the traditional end of the season pruning. It may only be effective in warmer locales. It is not for those of you growing doubles such as 'Walter Pennell' which bloom with double flowers only in the spring and then later produce single flowers. It is not for you if you are one of those gardeners who cannot live without their cute little seedheads. It also does not appear to work for clematis species.

The bottom line is if you would like to be on the cutting edge (pun intended), prune your clematis using this "Whack Attack" technique and you too may be rewarded with additional crops of blooms!

Clematis seedheads

TIDYING TIPS AND PRUNING POINTERS

♦ Use a pair of **sharp** clippers.
Have a pail for debris and plastic-covered wire ties on hand.
♦ It is important to take your time and be patient.
♦ Always start at the top of the stem and work your way down. This eliminates accidentally cutting off too much of a live stem. You can identify a live stem by cutting off a small piece near its top. A live stem will still be greenish inside.
♦ If your clematis is a tangled mess you can't unravel, prune just below the problem area. Be brave, this will be painful but necessary. Spread out the remaining stems and re-attach them to their support structure.
♦ Routinely remove and discard dead, injured or diseased stems and leaves throughout the growing season.
♦ Remove the old plastic tape that the wholesale nursery used because this is a perfect insect haven!
♦ Spray clippers with a solution of horticultural disinfectant after each cut to prevent the spread of fungal diseases.
♦ After pruning, spray the plant with a horticultural oil to kill any overwintering insects and eggs residing on the remaining stems.

CLEMATIS AND THEIR SENTIMENTS

Assigning special meanings to flowers is known as Floriography. The language of flowers has long been part of social customs but it was at the height of fashion during the Victorian era. In the 19th century special guidebooks were developed to identify the symbolic meaning of flowers. These flower codes allowed lovers to silently communicate their feelings during strict times when many sentiments were not permitted.

Clematis were most often assigned the meaning of "mental beauty" so if you were to add a clematis bloom to a bouquet, you would be revealing "I love your mind." Clematis were occasionally defined as "filial love", meaning a son's or daughter's love toward his or her parent. An evergreen clematis conveyed "poverty".

CLEMATIS AS CUT FLOWERS

Most of us know how lovely clematis are in the garden but they also make an ideal choice for cut flowers. Their beautiful blooms will brighten any room in your home. Large-flowered cultivars, *Clematis viticella* cultivars and *Clematis* x *durandii* are some of the best candidates for cut flowers because their flowers can last up to two weeks, depending on which variety is selected.

HARVESTING & CONDITIONING CUT CLEMATIS

When cutting clematis, always gather them either early in the morning or in the evening. These are the times when they will be at their freshest, since their stems are fully hydrated. For longest-lasting flowers, select clematis blooms that are just beginning to open (up to 70%). Remove any leaves that would be covered by water to prevent decay. Re-cut green stems and split the woody stems with a clean sharp floral knife (preferable) or clippers. Make your cuts on a 45 degree angle. Dip the stem ends into boiling water for 10 seconds. Place the newly cut flowers into a three-quarters full container of warm water. Add a floral preservative to help prevent bacterial growth. Let the flowers rejuvenate overnight in a cool dark place before arranging them.

MAKING THE MOST OF YOUR CUT CLEMATIS

Although the most time honored way of using cut clematis flowers is floating them in a bowl, they also look spectacular arranged in a vase or incorporated into floral arrangements. To ensure that they last as long as possible you should recondition them every two to three days. Re-cut the stems, change the water, add a flower preservative and enjoy.

KEY TO THE PORTRAIT PAGES

CLEMATIS NAME

CULTIVARS. The term **cultivar** is short for cultivated variety. These are plants that are grown in gardens and do not occur naturally in the wild. Cultivars do not come true from seed. They are replicated by human intervention (i.e. maintained in cultivation by mankind) because of their desirable characteristics. Cultivar names are designated by single quotation marks and are always capitalized. An example of this would be the cultivar 'Gipsy Queen'.

NATIVE SPECIES. These are plants that grow naturally in the wild. They can reproduce themselves in nature by breeding with one another and when grown from seed are normally true to their parents. Species is the second word in the botanical or Latin name and is written in lower case and *italicized*. The singular use of species is also referred to as species. The species name is often an adjective describing the genus name *Clematis*. It can tell you what color its flower is, its smell, its origin, or growth habits etc. An example would be *Clematis crispa*. *Crispa* is derived from the Latin word(s) crispa, crispum, crispus which means curled or wavy.

SYNONYMS (SYN.). This indicates that there are two or more names in commerce or a widely accepted misspelling. Synonyms can also describe the duplicated name that is already in existence of a plant that has since had to be renamed.

DATE OF INTRODUCTION. This is the year when the clematis was first presented to the gardening public. It is located in parentheses under the plant's name. Example:{1881}. When the date of introduction is unknown or uncertain, it is omitted.

C. 'Marie Boisselot' with climbing miniature *Rosa* 'Candy Cane'.

43

PRONUNCIATION. Clematis names can often be intimidating to pronounce. I have included the pronunciations of clematis names that may not be obvious. Remember, just like the infamous word CLEM-uh-tis, there may be other interpretations of the correct pronunciation.

HERITAGE

HYBRIDIZER. The hybridizer is the name of the person who first cultivated the clematis.

DISCOVERER. Clematis are sometimes discovered instead of bred. People who discovered a clematis are given recognition.

COUNTRY OF ORIGIN. This identifies the country in which a clematis was originally raised.

PARENTAGE. When the names of the two clematis parent plants used in breeding a cultivar are known, an "x" indicates the crossing of those two parents. An example of this would be *Clematis* 'Charissima' which is a cross between *C.* 'Kathleen Wheeler' x *C.* 'Nelly Moser'. If only one parent is known it is listed as a chance seedling of the known parent. For example, *Clematis* 'Gillian Blades' has the identified parent of *Clematis* 'Lasurstern' and is listed as a seedling of *C.* 'Lasurstern'. If a clematis is a sport it is listed as such. When neither parent is known it is listed as unknown.

GROWING ZONES

All the clematis selected for this book grow in USDA Zones 4 thru 11. Characteristics of certain plants may vary from zone to zone and are pointed out in their portraits.

BLOOMING PERIOD

I intentionally avoid using the specific season names of spring, summer, fall and winter in this book when it comes to blooming periods. I instead use the terms "early in the season", "mid season" and "late in the season" and those phrases address the first blooming period you experience in your particular growing zone. These phrases pertain to what I would consider a normal spring through a normal summer season. I have taken this approach because seasonal characteristics can

44

dramatically vary from zone to zone as well as year to year and normal is a subjective term. Therefore I have left it up to you to determine what is normal for your specific area. When I suggest that a clematis may repeat later in the season it means that this particular variety has the ability to produce more than one crop of blooms throughout the year. When and if these subsequent crops occur depends upon the variety of clematis and its locale.

HEIGHT RANGE. In regard to the height of a clematis, realize that these are only estimated heights and, in most cases, I try to err on the shorter side. The reason I have taken this approach is because should a clematis not reach its designated height, the gardener becomes disappointed. On the other hand, some gardeners have bionic yards and everything they plant grows larger than what is normally expected. So, as you read this book, keep in mind that height ranges are only meant to be an approximation.

LIGHT EXPOSURE. Most clematis prefer a full-sun location. This means they require five to six hours of sunlight for optimum blooming performance. Shady locations are best suited for delicate-colored clematis, especially the light-pink and soft silvery-lavender cultivars. Those varieties do best when planted in *bright* shade. This *bright* shade consists of areas that experience partial shade or dappled shade, but never receive direct, continuous sunlight. Direct sunlight bleaches the soft colors of these pale clematis's flowers, leaving them a dingy, washed-out gray. Bright shady locations are also recommended for extremely hot areas of this country where the scorching summer heat can burn clematis blooms.

PRUNING. The types of pruning are light, hard and optional. See the Pruning section in this book for more details.

HIGHLIGHTS
This emphasizes interesting features and uses for each clematis.

ANECDOTAL
These anecdotes provide interesting observations pertaining to an individual clematis.

FLOWER SIZE. The dimensions used in this book reflect the first crop of blooms. Subsequent crops of flowers can be smaller than the first crop.

COLOR. The description of color is purely subjective. For that reason I believe it is imperative to have a color picture to refer to. What I might think is more blue than lavender another might feel is more lavender than blue. So keep that in mind when reading the color descriptions.

Clematis blooms range in color from white, yellow, pink and mauve to crimson, lavender and purple. There are *no* "true blue" clematis even though they are often inaccurately described that way. For example, *Clematis* 'Perle d'Azur' is attributed to be colored "sky blue." The last time I looked at the sky it was not that shade of lavender-blue. *Clematis* 'H.F. Young' is described as "Wedgwood blue". If you own a piece of Wedgwood china, compare it with the coloring of your 'H.F. Young' the next time it blooms and you will see my point.

Even though many gardeners may long for them, "true blue" flowers are one of the rarest commodities in nature. I do not want to disappoint anyone reading my book when I use the word "blue" in describing a

clematis, so when I use the word "blue", I am referring to a shade of periwinkle or a secondary blue hue in the flower. I never mean to imply that the flower is truly blue because there is always more lavender or purple (sometimes violet) in its coloring.

This also holds true for the color red. There are no "true red" clematis. So when you see the word "red", be aware of the fact that the flower has a blue hue which can give it a magenta cast.

C. H. F. Young

C. 'Belle of Woking' with *Rosa* 'Dortmund'.

Clematis 'Aotearoa'

{1995}

PRONUNCIATION

Ah-o-tay-a-<u>row</u>-ah

HERITAGE
Hybridizer: Alister Keay
Country of Origin: New Zealand
Parentage: Unknown

GROWING ZONES
USDA Growing Zones 4 thru 11.

BLOOMING PERIOD
In USDA Zones 4 thru 9 later in the season and may repeat.
In USDA Zones 10 & 11 early in the season and repeats.

Height Range: Six to nine feet.
Light Exposure: It thrives equally in sunny
or shady locations.
Pruning: Optional or hard.

.

HIGHLIGHTS
This lovely New Zealand clematis is perfect for a tall obelisk.
It produces masses of stunning flowers and is easy to grow.

ANECDOTAL
Aotearoa means "Land of the long white cloud" and is
the name the Maori people use for New Zealand. The
Maori are the indigenous people of New Zealand.

C. 'Aotearoa'

FLOWER FEATURES AND PLANT CHARACTERISTICS

The flower's tepals are a rich dark purple. The flower is
4" to 5" in diameter and has 6 pointed tepals.
Its stamens are yellow.

Clematis 'Asao'

PRONUNCIATION
As-<u>sow</u>

HERITAGE
Hybridizer: Kazushige Ozawa
Country of Origin: Japan
Parentage: Unknown

GROWING ZONES
USDA Growing Zones 4 thru 11.

BLOOMING PERIOD
Early in the season and repeats.

Height Range: Six to eight feet.
Light Exposure: It is best planted in an area with some
shade to prevent the flowers from fading.
Pruning: Optional or light.

HIGHLIGHTS
This eye-catching clematis is seasonally an early bloomer.
It is a nice compact plant that will grow moderately.
It is a perfect clematis for growing in a container.

ANECDOTAL
Asao is the name of the town where this plant's
hybridizer, Kazushige Ozawa, resides. In the past,
Asao was a popular name for ladies in
Japanese high society.

C. 'Asao'

FLOWER FEATURES AND PLANT CHARACTERISTICS
The flower's tepals are a deep rosy-pink with a white bar in the
center. The flower is 4" to 6" in diameter and has 6 to 7 tepals.
Its stamens are yellow.

Clematis 'Ascotiensis'

{1874}

PRONUNCIATION
As-co-tee-<u>en</u>-sis

HERITAGE
Hybridizer: John Standish
Country of Origin: United Kingdom
Parentage: Unknown

GROWING ZONES
USDA Growing Zones 4 thru 11.

BLOOMING PERIOD
In USDA Zones 4 thru 9 later in the season and may repeat.
In USDA Zones 10 & 11 early in the season and repeats.

Height Range: Seven to ten feet.
Light Exposure: It thrives equally in sunny
or shady locations.
Pruning: Optional or hard.

HIGHLIGHTS
This excellent climber makes a good choice for an arbor.
Matching an 'Ascotiensis' with a yellow rose would make
a wonderful combination. It is vigorous and
a dependable performer.

ANECDOTAL
'Ascotiensis' is named after the location where it was
raised, Ascot, in the United Kingdom, where it blooms in
time for the Royal Ascot Races.

C. 'Ascotiensis'

FLOWER FEATURES AND PLANT CHARACTERISTICS
The flower's tepals are a bright lavender-blue. The flower
is 5" in diameter and has 4 to 6 broad tepals.
Its stamens are a pale green.

Clematis 'Barbara Dibley'

{1949}

PRONUNCIATION
Dib-lee

HERITAGE
Hybridizer: G. Rowland Jackman
Country of Origin: United Kingdom
Parentage: Unknown

GROWING ZONES
USDA Growing Zones 4 thru 11.

BLOOMING PERIOD
Early in the season and repeats.

Height Range: Up to six feet.
Light Exposure: In hotter locales it is best to plant it in
an area with some shade to prevent the flowers from fading.
Pruning: Optional or light.

HIGHLIGHTS
Grow this clematis for its unbelievable breathtaking coloring.
It is a very compact plant making it perfect for
a short obelisk.

ANECDOTAL
Clematis 'Barbara Dibley' is the namesake of
Mr. Jackman's secretary.

C. 'Barbara Dibley'

FLOWER FEATURES AND PLANT CHARACTERISTICS
The flower's tepals are a striking raspberry-pink with an intense carmine stripe. The flower is 6" to 8" in diameter and produces 6 to 8 rippled, undulating tepals.
Its stamens are a reddish-brown color.

Clematis 'Barbara Jackman'

{1952}

HERITAGE
Hybridizer: G. Rowland Jackman
Country of Origin: United Kingdom
Parentage: Unknown

GROWING ZONES
USDA Growing Zones 4 thru 11.

BLOOMING PERIOD
Early in the season and repeats.

Height Range: Six to eight feet.
Light Exposure: It thrives equally in sunny
or shady locations.
Pruning: Optional or light.

HIGHLIGHTS
This captivating clematis can shine on its own or can be
combined with other striking clematis such as *C.* 'Piilu'
for a to-die-for combination. Attractively decorates
medium sized obelisks or trellises.

ANECDOTAL
Mr. Jackman named this clematis after his
wife, Barbara.

C. 'Barbara Jackman'

FLOWER FEATURES AND PLANT CHARACTERISTICS
The flower's tepals are deep purple with a vivid magenta bar. The flower is 5" to 6" in diameter and has 8 broadly overlapping tepals. Its stamens are creamy yellow.

Clematis 'Bees Jubilee'

{1958}

PRONUNCIATION
Bees Ju-bi-<u>lee</u>

HERITAGE
Hybridizer: Bees Ltd. Nurseries
Country of Origin: United Kingdom
Parentage: Unknown

GROWING ZONES
USDA Growing Zones 4 thru 11.

BLOOMING PERIOD
Early in the season and repeats.

Height Range: Six to eight feet.
Light Exposure: In hotter locales it is best to plant it in an
area with some shade to prevent the flowers from fading.
Pruning: Optional or light.

HIGHLIGHTS
It is often described as a more vivid version of
'Nelly Moser'. It will brighten a shady corner.
It is a compact clematis that
does well in containers.

ANECDOTAL
Not to be mistaken for our honey producing,
pollinating garden friend, Mr. Bees named this clematis
to commemorate the celebration of the
25th anniversary of his nursery.

C. 'Bees Jubilee'

FLOWER FEATURES AND PLANT CHARACTERISTICS
The flower's tepals are a pretty mauve-pink with a rosy
carmine bar. The flower is 6" to 8" in diameter and
has 6 to 8 flat, rounded, overlapping tepals.
Its stamens are light brown.

Clematis 'Belle Nantaise'

{1887}

PRONUNCIATION
Bell Non-<u>tez</u>

HERITAGE
Hybridizer: Auguste Boisselot
Country of Origin: France
Parentage: Unknown

GROWING ZONES
USDA Growing Zones 4 thru 11.

BLOOMING PERIOD
Early in the season and repeats.

Height Range: Six to nine feet.
Light Exposure: It thrives equally in sunny
or shady locations.
Pruning: Optional or light.

HIGHLIGHTS
Grow this clematis for its exceptionally large dinner-plate
blossoms and very prominent stamens. A dependable
cultivar for its free-flowering ability, it would look
lovely in a cottage garden setting.

ANECDOTAL
The word "belle" means beautiful and "nantaise"
translates to "inhabitants of Nantes", a city in western
France, and home to Mr. Boisselot.

C. 'Belle Nantaise'

FLOWER FEATURES AND PLANT CHARACTERISTICS
The flower's tepals are a delicate lavender-blue. The
flower is 7" to 9" in diameter and has 6 very large tepals.
Its stamens are a cream color.

Clematis 'Belle of Woking'

{1881}

PRONUNCIATION
Bell of <u>Woe</u>-king

HERITAGE
Hybridizer: George Jackman & Son
Country of Origin: United Kingdom
Parentage: *C. lanuginosa* 'Candida' x *C.* 'Fortunei'

GROWING ZONES
USDA Growing Zones 4 thru 11.

BLOOMING PERIOD
Early in the season and repeats.

Height Range: Six to nine feet.
Light Exposure: It thrives equally in sunny
or shady locations.
Pruning: Optional or light.

HIGHLIGHTS
Charming and elegant, this clematis consistently doubles,
putting on a beautiful show. It is stunning when
combined with a contrasting red rose
such as 'Dortmund.'

ANECDOTAL
Woking in Surrey, England was the location of the
famous nursery of the renowned clematis legend,
George Jackman.

C. 'Belle of Woking'

FLOWER FEATURES AND PLANT CHARACTERISTICS
The flower's tepals create a pretty double flower. They are colored a silvery-mauve that quickly fades to a silvery-gray. The flower is 4" in diameter and forms a neat dome-shaped rosette.
Its stamens are cream colored.

Clematis 'Bill MacKenzie'

(syn. *C. orientalis* 'Bill MacKenzie' or
C. tangutica 'Bill MacKenzie')

{circa 1969}

HERITAGE
Hybridizer: Unknown
Country of Origin: United Kingdom
Parentage: Unknown

GROWING ZONES
USDA Growing Zones 4 thru 11.

BLOOMING PERIOD
Mid to late season.

Height Range:
7 to 10 feet in USDA Zones 10 & 11
Up to 20 feet in USDA Zones 4 thru 9.
Light Exposure: It thrives equally in sunny
or shady locations.
Pruning: Optional or hard.

HIGHLIGHTS
In the autumn, after a show of dainty flowers, this
standout clematis is covered with masses of fluffy
silver-colored seedheads which are excellent to use in
Thanksgiving floral arrangements.

ANECDOTAL
According to the distinguished clematarian, Wim Snoeijer,
'Bill MacKenzie' was discovered as a chance
seedling at the Waterperry Horticultural College,
near Oxford, UK, around 1969.

C. 'Bill MacKenzie'

FLOWER FEATURES AND PLANT CHARACTERISTICS

The flower's tepals are a bright mustard-yellow and form sweet lantern-shaped flowers. The flower is 1½" to 2" in diameter and has 4 tepals that are said to resemble orange peel because of their waxy-textured surface. Its stamens are reddish-brown.

Clematis 'Blue Gem'

{1875}

HERITAGE
Hybridizer: George Jackman & Son
Country of Origin: United Kingdom
Parentage: *C. lanuginosa* x *C.* 'Standishii'

GROWING ZONES
USDA Growing Zones 4 thru 11.

BLOOMING PERIOD
Early in the season and repeats.

Height Range: Six to eight feet.
Light Exposure: It thrives equally in sunny
or shady locations.
Pruning: Optional or hard.

HIGHLIGHTS
This jewel of a clematis is a very dependable old
cultivar. It definitely deserves more recognition.
It makes a wonderful choice for
a mixed border.

C. 'Blue Gem'

The flower's tepals are large and an attractive lavender-blue. The flower is 5" to 7" in diameter and has 6 to 8 overlapping tepals. Its stamens are reddish-brown.

Clematis 'Blue Light'

(syn. *C.* 'Vanso')

{Circa 1998}

HERITAGE
Hybridizer: Frans van Haasterd
Country of Origin: Holland
Parentage: A sport of *C.* 'Mrs Cholmondeley'

GROWING ZONES
USDA Growing Zones 4 thru 11.

BLOOMING PERIOD
Early in the season and repeats.

Height Range: Up to six feet.
Light Exposure: It thrives equally in sunny
or shady locations.
Pruning: Optional or light.

HIGHLIGHTS
This beguiling clematis is definitely an
attention-getter. It has tremendous longevity as
a cut flower and is highly suitable
for containers.

C. 'Blue Light'

FLOWER FEATURES AND PLANT CHARACTERISTICS
The flower's tepals create a striking double flower. They are colored a pastel lavender-blue. The flower is 3" to 4" in diameter and consists of 6 to 8 outer tepals and a central cluster of tepals that resemble a pompom. As it ages the outer tepals drop off making its "pompom resemblance" even more pronounced. Its stamens are not visible.

Clematis 'C. W. Dowman'

<u>Dow</u>-man

HERITAGE
Hybridizer: Walter Pennell
Country of Origin: United Kingdom
Parentage: Unknown

GROWING ZONES
USDA Growing Zones 4 thru 11.

BLOOMING PERIOD
Early in the season and repeats.

Height Range: Six to eight feet.
Light Exposure: It is best planted in an area with
some shade to prevent the flowers from fading.
Pruning: Optional or light.

HIGHLIGHTS
Another beautiful two-tone clematis for the shade.
'C. W. Dowman' is significantly more demure than
other pale, barred varieties. It makes a nice
container selection.

ANECDOTAL
In 1961, this clematis was named after a loyal
employee of the Pennells' nursery, Mr. Dowman,
who was involved with hybridization.

C. 'C. W. Dowman'

The flower's tepals are colored a pale pink with a carmine bar.
The flower is 6" to 8" in diameter and has 6 to 8 tepals.
Its stamens are a creamy-yellow.

Clematis 'Carnaby'

{1983}

PRONUNCIATION
Kar-na-bee

HERITAGE
Hybridizer: Unknown
Country of Origin: U.S.A.
Parentage: Unknown

GROWING ZONES
USDA Growing Zones 4 thru 11.

Blooming Period
Early in the season and repeats.

Height Range: Four to six feet.
Light Exposure: In hotter locales its best planted in an area
with some shade to prevent the flowers from fading.
Pruning: Optional or light.

HIGHLIGHTS
Spellbinding coloring and a chance to preserve our American
heritage makes it a great choice. Its compact size makes it
perfect for containers.

ANECDOTAL
This is the first American large-flowering hybrid. Even
though it originated in the U.S. it was Treasures of Tenbury
that is credited for introducing it. Treasures of Tenbury,
which is located in England, houses a national
collection of clematis.

C. 'Carnaby'

FLOWER FEATURES AND PLANT CHARACTERISTICS

The flower's tepals are a strikingly intense magenta and are edged with pink or white. The flower is 6" to 8" in diameter and has 6 tepals that are overlapping. Its stamens are maroon-brown.

Clematis 'Charissima'

PRONUNCIATION
Ka-<u>riss</u>-see-ma

HERITAGE
Hybridizer: Walter Pennell
Country of Origin: United Kingdom
Parentage: *C.* 'Kathleen Wheeler' x *C.* 'Nelly Moser'

GROWING ZONES
USDA Growing Zones 4 thru 11.

BLOOMING PERIOD
Early in the season and repeats.

Height Range: Six to eight feet.
Light Exposure: In hotter locales its best planted in an area
with some shade to prevent the flowers from fading.
Pruning: Optional or light.

HIGHLIGHTS
An alluringly beautiful two-toned clematis, 'Charissima'
definitely has charisma. It makes a nice choice to brighten
a shady location.

ANECDOTAL
Walter Pennell raised this clematis in 1961. He wanted to
pay tribute to a loyal employee, Sheila Gilbert, by naming
this clematis after her. She graciously declined and requested
that it be named Charissima.

C. 'Charissima'

FLOWER FEATURES AND PLANT CHARACTERISTICS

The flower's tepals are a striking cerise-pink with a deeper pink bar. The flower is 6" to 8" in diameter and has 6 to 8 tepals. Its stamens are reddish-brown.

Clematis 'Colette Deville'

{1898}

PRONUNCIATION
Co-<u>let</u> Duh-<u>veel</u>

HERITAGE
Hybridizer: André Leroy
Country of Origin: France
Parentage: Unknown

GROWING ZONES
USDA Growing Zones 4 thru 11.

BLOOMING PERIOD
Early in the season and repeats.

Height Range: Six to eight feet.
Light Exposure: It thrives equally in sunny
or shady locations.
Pruning: Optional or light.

HIGHLIGHTS
This venerable French clematis provides the garden
with a magnificent shade of crimson coloring. It would
be a good choice to grow into a small shrub such as
Spiraea x bumalda.

C. 'Colette Deville'

FLOWER FEATURES AND PLANT CHARACTERISTICS
The flower's tepals are a stunning mauvish-red. The flower
is 6" in diameter and has 6 to 8 narrow tepals.
Its stamens are reddish-brown.

Clematis 'Comtesse de Bouchaud'

(syn. often misspelled *C.* 'Comtesse de Bouchard')

{1900}

PRONUNCIATION
Con-<u>tes</u> duh Boo-<u>show</u>

HERITAGE
Hybridizer: Frances (Francisque) Morel
Country of Origin: France
Parentage: Unknown

GROWING ZONES
USDA Growing Zones 4 thru 11.

BLOOMING PERIOD
In USDA Zones 4 thru 9 later in the season and may repeat.
In USDA Zones 10 & 11 late in the season and repeats.

Height Range: Six to eight feet.
Light Exposure: It thrives equally in sunny
or shady locations.
Pruning: Optional or hard.

HIGHLIGHTS
This is a prolific bloomer, making it a very popular
clematis. Because of its compact nature it is perfect
to grow in a container.

ANECDOTAL
This French clematis was named in honor of an
aristocrat's wife. Comtesse is the
French word for countess.

C. 'Comtesse de Bouchaud'

FLOWER FEATURES AND PLANT CHARACTERISTICS
The flower's tepals are a bright velvety-pink with
marked midribs. The flower is 4" to 6" in
diameter and has 6 tepals.
Its stamens are cream colored.

Clematis crispa

(common name: Swamp Leather Flower)

PRONUNCIATION
<u>kris</u>-pa

HERITAGE
Country of Origin: U.S.A.
Parentage: A native species

GROWING ZONES
USDA Growing Zones 4 thru 11.

BLOOMING PERIOD
In USDA Zones 4 thru 9 later in the season and may repeat.
In USDA Zones 10 & 11 early in the season and repeats
throughout the year.

Height Range: Five to eight feet.
Light Exposure: It thrives equally in sunny or shady locations.
Pruning: Hard. It dies to the ground in the colder zones.

HIGHLIGHTS
C. crispa is a must for serious clematis aficionados. Despite
its delicate appearance, it is quite a prolific bloomer. It is a
semi-woody climber that produces charming little bell-shaped
blooms. Since *C. crispa* is such a delicate and slender vine it would
be beneficial to plant it with other shrubs to help support it.
It has a very long blooming period.

ANECDOTAL
Clematis crispa was introduced in England in 1726 (possibly
even before that date). I have not found any records of American
species cited before then, so I will presume it is the very
first American clematis species.

C. crispa

FLOWER FEATURES AND PLANT CHARACTERISTICS
The flower's tepals are colored a dainty pale lavender-blue. They
form a sweet nodding bell with flared tips. The flower is 1" to
1½" in diameter and has 4 tepals that are lightly ribbed.
It stamens are a cream yellow.

Clematis 'Daniel Deronda'

{circa 1882}

PRONUNCIATION
De-<u>ron</u>-da

HERITAGE
Hybridizer: Charles Noble
Country of Origin: United Kingdom
Parentage: Possibly *C. patens* x *C. lanuginosa*

GROWING ZONES
USDA Growing Zones 4 thru 11.

BLOOMING PERIOD
Early in the season and repeats.

Height Range: Six to eight feet.
Light Exposure: It thrives equally in sunny
or shady locations.
Pruning: Optional or light.

HIGHLIGHTS
Often overlooked, this truly is a spectacular clematis.
Its remarkable coloring makes it a hit in any garden.
Occasionally the flowers can be semi-double in
spring in USDA Zones 4 thru 9.

ANECDOTAL
Mr. Noble raised this cultivar that is named after the
character in George Eliot's final book.

C. 'Daniel Deronda'

FLOWER FEATURES AND PLANT CHARACTERISTICS
The flower's tepals are a strikingly deep violet-blue.
The flower is 6" to 8" in diameterand has 8
overlapping pointed tepals.
Its stamens are a contrasting ivory color.

Clematis 'Dawn'

{1969}

Heritage
Discoverer: Tage Lundell
Country of Origin: Sweden
Parentage: Possibly a seedling of *C.* 'Moonlight' x *C.* 'Nelly Moser'.

Growing Zones
USDA Growing Zones 4 thru 11.

Blooming Period
Early in the season and repeats.

Height Range: Up to six feet.
Light Exposure: Its best planted in an area with some
shade to prevent the flowers from fading.
Pruning: Optional or light.

Highlights
Just like the first blush of day this sweet clematis
brightens a shady garden. This compact clematis does
well in containers.

Anecdotal
Mr. Lundell changed the name to 'Dawn' after
discovering that his first choice, "Aurora",
had already been taken.

C. 'Dawn'

FLOWER FEATURES AND PLANT CHARACTERISTICS
The flower's tepals are a subtle pearly-pink. The flower
is 5" in diameter and has 6 to 8 tepals.
Its stamens are reddish-brown.

Clematis 'Dorothy Tolver'

{1993}

PRONUNCIATION
<u>Toll</u>-ver or <u>Tall</u>-ver

HERITAGE
Hybridizer: Jonathan Gooch
Country of Origin: United Kingdom
Parentage: *C.* 'Niobe' x *C.* 'Vyvyan Pennell'

GROWING ZONES
USDA Growing Zones 4 thru 11.

BLOOMING PERIOD
Early in the season and repeats.

Height Range: Six to eight feet.
Light Exposure: It thrives equally in sunny
or shady locations.
Pruning: Optional or light.

HIGHLIGHTS
Totally irresistible because of its unique pink coloring,
'Dorothy Tolver' may occasionally produce double
flowers in USDA Zones 4 thru 9.

ANECDOTAL
Nurseryman Jonathan Gooch named this clematis
after his mother-in-law.

C. 'Dorothy Tolver'

<small>FLOWER FEATURES AND PLANT CHARACTERISTICS</small>
The flower's tepals are a vibrant mauve-pink. The flower
is 4" to 6" in diameter and has 6 tepals.
Its stamens are yellow.

Clematis 'Duchess of Edinburgh'

{1874}

PRONUNCIATION
Dutch-ess of Ed-in-bur-ra

HERITAGE
Hybridizer: George Jackman & Son
Country of Origin: United Kingdom
Parentage: Unknown

GROWING ZONES
USDA Growing Zones 4 thru 11.

BLOOMING PERIOD
Early in the season and repeats.

Height Range: Six to eight feet.
Light Exposure: It thrives equally in sunny
or shady locations.
Pruning: Optional or light.

HIGHLIGHTS
It is one of the very best doubles to grace your garden
because of the countless pretty, creamy-white flowers.
It also has one of the longest lasting blooms.
It is a fabulous clematis for
small gardens.

ANECDOTAL
One of the earliest known double clematis.

C. 'Duchess of Edinburgh'

FLOWER FEATURES AND PLANT CHARACTERISTICS
The flower's tepals form an elegant double rosette and are
colored white. The outermost skirt of the tepals edges
are touched with green. The flower is normally
4" in diameter, sometimes reaching up to 6".
Its stamens are cream-colored.

Clematis x *durandii*

(syn. *C. integrifolia* 'Durandii' or *C.* 'Durandii')

{1870}

PRONUNCIATION
duh-<u>randy</u>-eye

HERITAGE
Hybridizer: Durand Frères
Country of Origin: France
Parentage: *C. integrifolia* x *C. lanuginosa*

GROWING ZONES
USDA Growing Zones 4 thru 11.

BLOOMING PERIOD
Mid season and may repeat.

Height Range: 3 to 5 feet.
Light Exposure: It thrives equally in sunny
or shady locations.
Pruning: Hard. It will die to the ground in the
colder zones.

HIGHLIGHTS
Durandii are non-clinging clematis so they need support
as they grow. This can be achieved by allowing them to grow
into another shrub as a support. It is a very vigorous and
free-flowering clematis. It makes a good container
selection as well as being a fabulous cut flower.

C. x *durandii*

FLOWER FEATURES AND PLANT CHARACTERISTICS
The flower's tepals are colored an indigo-blue. The flower is
4" in diameter and usually has 4 (though may sometimes
produce 5 or 6) tepals with deep-channeled midribs.
Its stamens are golden-yellow.

Clematis 'Elsa Späth'

{1891}

PRONUNCIATION
El-sa <u>spayth</u>

HERITAGE
Hybridizer: L. Späth
Country of Origin: Germany
Parentage: Unknown

GROWING ZONES
USDA Growing Zones 4 thru 11.

BLOOMING PERIOD
Early in the season and repeats.

Height Range: Six to eight feet.
Light Exposure: It thrives equally in sunny
or shady locations.
Pruning: Optional or light.

HIGHLIGHTS
Popular because it is an easy clematis to grow and produces
nicely shaped flowers for a very long period of time. It
is a perfect clematis for a container or pot.

C. 'Elsa Späth'

FLOWER FEATURES AND PLANT CHARACTERISTICS
The flower's tepals are colored a rich violet-blue. The
flower is 6" to 8" in diameter and has 6 to 8 very
rounded and overlapping tepals.
Its stamens are reddish-brown.

Clematis 'Ernest Markham'

{1938}

PRONUNCIATION
Mar-kum

HERITAGE
Hybridizer: Ernest Markham
Country of Origin: United Kingdom
Parentage: Unknown

GROWING ZONES
USDA Growing Zones 4 thru 11.

BLOOMING PERIOD
In USDA Zones 4 thru 9 later in the season and may repeat.
In USDA Zones 10 & 11 early in the season and repeats.

Height Range: Six to nine feet.
Light Exposure: It thrives equally in sunny or shady locations.
Pruning: Optional or hard.

HIGHLIGHTS
This modern classic boasts of an outstanding flowering
ability. One of the most popular red clematis, it is known for
producing profusions of flowers. It is an excellent selection
for novice gardeners because it is durable as well as
being easy to grow.

ANECDOTAL
Ernest Markham is a renowned clematarian and the author
of a book about clematis. Rowland Jackman named it
after Ernest, who was the head gardener for
William Robinson of Gravetye Manor.

C. 'Ernest Markham'

FLOWER FEATURES AND PLANT CHARACTERISTICS
The flower's tepals are colored a glowing magenta. The flower
is 4" to 6" in diameter and has 6 deeply textured tepals.
Its stamens are small and golden.

Clematis 'Etoile de Malicorne'

{circa 1969}

PRONUNCIATION
Ay-<u>twal</u> duh Molly-<u>corn</u>

HERITAGE
Hybridizer: A. Girault
Country of Origin: France
Parentage: Unknown

GROWING ZONES
USDA Growing Zones 4 thru 11.

BLOOMING PERIOD
Early in the season and repeats.

Height Range: Six to eight feet.
Light Exposure: It thrives equally in sunny
or shady locations.
Pruning: Optional or light.

HIGHLIGHTS
An easily grown French clematis with captivating coloring
combined with the fact that this striped cultivar can take
full sun makes it a plus in any garden. It does
well in a container.

ANECDOTAL
The name means "star of Malicorne." Malicorne
is a county in France, a last name and a
character in an Alexandre Dumas novel.

C. 'Etoile de Malicorne'

FLOWER FEATURES AND PLANT CHARACTERISTICS
The flower's tepals are a lovely lilac and have a magenta
bar. The flower is 6" to 8" in diameter and
has 6 to 8 rounded tepals.
Its stamens are reddish-brown.

Clematis 'Fairy Queen'

{1875}

HERITAGE
Hybridizer: Thomas Cripps & Son
Country of Origin: United Kingdom
Parentage: *C. lanuginosa* x *C. patens*

GROWING ZONES
USDA Growing Zones 4 thru 11.

BLOOMING PERIOD
Early in the season and repeats.

Height Range: Six to eight feet.
Light Exposure: Its best planted in an area with some
shade to prevent the flowers from fading
Pruning: Optional or light.

HIGHLIGHTS
This is an enchanting beauty with exceptionally large blossoms
that are bestowed with soft, alluring coloring. It is free
flowering and would make a welcome addition to any
shade garden. It is such a magnificent clematis, so it is a
shame that it is not more readily available.

C. 'Fairy Queen'

FLOWER FEATURES AND PLANT CHARACTERISTICS
The flower's tepals are colored pinkish-white and have a rosy-mauve bar. The flower can be 7" to 9" in diameter and has 8 very large tepals.Its stamens are dusty-purple.

Clematis 'General Sikorski'

{circa 1980}

PRONUNCIATION
General Si-<u>kor</u>-ski

HERITAGE
Hybridizer: Wladyslaw Noll
Country of Origin: Poland
Parentage: Unknown

GROWING ZONES
USDA GROWING ZONES 4 THRU 11.

BLOOMING PERIOD
Early in the season and repeats.

Height Range: Six to eight feet.
Light Exposure: It thrives equally in sunny
or shady locations.
Pruning: Optional or light.

HIGHLIGHTS
This Polish clematis gives you a delightful array
of soft periwinkle blossoms.

ANECDOTAL
Named for the Polish soldier and politician, General Wladyslaw
Sikorski (1881-1943). Side by side comparisons show that the
Clematis 'Jadwiga Teresa', which was raised by Brother Stefan
Franczak in 1965, is virtually identical to *C.* 'General Sikorski'.
Franczak sent *C.* 'Jadwiga Teresa' to Wladyslaw Noll in 1969
where he is believed to have renamed it after the famous
general. It was then introduced by Jim Fisk in the early 1980's.

C. 'General Sikorski'

FLOWER FEATURES AND PLANT CHARACTERISTICS
The flower's tepals are a lavender-blue with a hint of red at
the base of each tepal. The flower is 6" to 8" in diameter
and has 6 crenulated and slightly overlapping tepals.
Its stamens are golden.

Clematis 'Gillian Blades'

{1975}

PRONUNCIATION
Gill-ee-un

HERITAGE
Hybridizer: Jim Fisk
Country of Origin: United Kingdom
Parentage: A seedling of *C.* 'Lasurstern'

GROWING ZONES
USDA Growing Zones 4 thru 11.

BLOOMING PERIOD
Early in the season and repeats.

Height Range: Six to eight feet.
Light Exposure: In hotter locales it is best planted in an
area with some shade to prevent the flowers from fading.
Pruning: Optional or light.

HIGHLIGHTS
Gillian Blades is a beautiful and refined clematis. It is
a good choice for compact spaces. It also is a fabulous
clematis for bridal bouquets.

ANECDOTAL
Mr. Fisk named this prized clematis after one
of his secretaries.

C. 'Gillian Blades'

F LOWER F EATURES AND P LANT C HARACTERISTICS

The flower's tepals are colored a pure white but when they first open the tepals are brushed with a tinge of mauve. The flower is 6" to 8" in diameter and has 7 to 8 tepals that are ruffled on the edges and pointed at the tips.

Its stamens are yellow.

Clematis 'Gipsy Queen'
(syn. *C.* 'Gypsy Queen')

{1877}

HERITAGE
Hybridizer: Thomas Cripps & Son
Country of Origin: United Kingdom
Parentage: *C.* 'Jackmanii' x *C. patens*

GROWING ZONES
USDA Growing Zones 4 thru 11.

Blooming Period
In USDA Zones 4 thru 9 later in the season and may repeat.
In USDA Zones 10 & 11 later in the season and repeats.

Height Range: Eight to twelve feet.
Light Exposure: It thrives equally in sunny
or shady locations.
Pruning: Optional or hard.

HIGHLIGHTS
This clematis combines elegance, refinement and rich
coloring all in one plant. It is an excellent choice because
it is free-flowering with vigorous growth that can easily
scale a tall trellis.

ANECDOTAL
'Gipsy Queen' has been mistaken for 'Jackmanii' and is often
mislabeled but it can be easily identified by its unique
tapered tepals.

C. 'Gipsy Queen'

FLOWER FEATURES AND PLANT CHARACTERISTICS
The flower's tepals are colored a deep velvety-purple. The flower is 4" to 6" in diameter and has 6 tepals that have distinct cutouts. Its stamens are wine colored.

Clematis 'Guiding Star'

{circa 1866}

HERITAGE
Hybridizer: Thomas Cripps & Son
Country of Origin: United Kingdom
Parentage: A seedling of *C. lanuginosa*

GROWING ZONES
USDA Growing Zones 4 thru 11.

BLOOMING PERIOD
Early in the season and repeats.

Height Range: Six to eight feet.
Light Exposure: It thrives equally in sunny
or shady locations.
Pruning: Optional or light.

HIGHLIGHTS
The stunning good looks of this clematis are derived
from its rich purple coloring. It makes an excellent
choice for a small garden or container.

C. 'Guiding Star'

Flower Features and Plant Characteristics
The flower's tepals are colored a lovely deep-purple
with even deeper colored veins. The flower is 5" to 6"
in diameter and has 6 to 8 tepals.
Its stamens are reddish-brown.

Clematis 'H. F. Young'

{circa 1962}

HERITAGE
Hybridizer: Walter Pennell
Country of Origin: United Kingdom
Parentage: Unknown

GROWING ZONES
USDA Growing Zones 4 thru 11.

BLOOMING PERIOD
Early in the season and repeats.

Height Range: Six to nine feet.
Light Exposure: It thrives equally in sunny
or shady locations.
Pruning: Optional or light.

HIGHLIGHTS
A well-admired clematis because of its exceptional color
and free-flowering ability, 'H. F. Young' makes an excellent
choice for a container or a small patio garden.

ANECDOTAL
Often described as "Wedgwood" blue, it realistically is
more of a lavender color. Mr. Pennell named this clematis
after Horace F. Young, who was director of Pennell's
branch office in Grimsby.

C. 'H. F. Young'

FLOWER FEATURES AND PLANT CHARACTERISTICS
The flower's tepals are colored an appealing periwinkle-tinged mauve. The flower is 6" to 8" in diameter and has 8 wide overlapping tepals. Its stamens are cream-colored.

Clematis 'Hagley Hybrid'
(syn. *C.* 'Pink Chiffon')

{1956}

PRONUNCIATION
Hag-lee

HERITAGE
Hybridizer: Percy Picton
Country of Origin: United Kingdom
Parentage: Unknown

GROWING ZONES
USDA Growing Zones 4 thru 11.

BLOOMING PERIOD
In USDA Zones 4 thru 9 later in the season and may repeat.
In USDA Zones 10 & 11 early in the season and repeats.

Height Range: Six to eight feet.
Light Exposure: It thrives equally in sunny
or shady locations.
Pruning: Optional or hard.

HIGHLIGHTS
A very popular pink variety because of its outstanding
flowering capability, this reliable clematis fades nicely
when grown in the sun. It is easy to grow and is a
great choice for a container.

ANECDOTAL
Raised by Percy Picton circa 1945 when he was
head gardener at Hagley Hall.

C. 'Hagley Hybrid'

FLOWER FEATURES AND PLANT CHARACTERISTICS
The flower's tepals are colored a dusky shell-pink. The flower is 4" to 6" in diameter and has 6 pointed, boat-shaped tepals. Its stamens are reddish-brown.

Clematis 'Henryi'

(syn. *C.* 'Henryii')

{1870}

PRONUNCIATION
<u>Hen</u>-ree-eye

HERITAGE
Hybridizer: Isaac Anderson-Henry
Country of Origin: Scotland
Parentage: *C. lanuginosa* x *C.* 'Fortunei'

GROWING ZONES
USDA Growing Zones 4 thru 11.

BLOOMING PERIOD
Early in the season and repeats.

Height Range: Six to nine feet.
Light Exposure: It thrives equally in sunny
or shady locations.
Pruning: Optional or light.

HIGHLIGHTS
This clematis has withstood the test of time, remaining
very popular today. It produces enormous white flowers
that are enhanced by the crown of its
contrasting dark stamens.

ANECDOTAL
This Scottish clematis, having been raised in 1855,
boasts the legacy of being one of the
oldest hybridized clematis.

C. 'Henryi'

FLOWER FEATURES AND PLANT CHARACTERISTICS
The flower's tepals are colored a distinct creamy-white. The
flower is 6" to 9" in diameter and has 8 pointed tepals
that overlap. Its stamens are coffee-colored.

Clematis 'Honora'

{1998}

O-<u>no</u>ra

HERITAGE
Discoverer: Mrs. A. Edwards
Country of Origin: New Zealand
Parentage: May be a sport of *C.* 'Gipsy Queen'

GROWING ZONES
USDA Growing Zones 4 thru 11.

BLOOMING PERIOD
In USDA Zones 4 thru 9 later in the season and may repeat.
In USDA Zones 10 & 11 later in the season and repeats.

Height Range: Six to eight feet.
Light Exposure: It thrives equally in sunny
or shady locations.
Pruning: Optional or hard.

HIGHLIGHTS
A relatively new introduction with very distinct coloring, its
dark stamens practically disappear into the flower. 'Honora's
blooms remain on the plant for long periods of time.
This beauty is destined to become a classic.

ANECDOTAL
Mrs. Edwards of Christchurch, New Zealand, called it
'Honora', a native Maori name. It was later introduced
by Alister Keay.

C. 'Honora'

The flower's tepals are a velvety raspberry-purple. The
flower is 5" to 7" in diameter and has 6 tepals.
Its stamens are reddish-purple.

Clematis 'Huldine'

{1934}

PRONUNCIATION
<u>Who'll</u> dean

HERITAGE
Hybridizer: Frances (Francisque) Morel
Country of Origin: France
Parentage: Unknown

GROWING ZONES
USDA Growing Zones 4 thru 11.

BLOOMING PERIOD
In USDA Zones 4 thru 9 later in the season and may repeat.
In USDA Zones 10 & 11 early in the season and repeats.

Height Range: Eight to ten (possibly fifteen) feet.
Light Exposure: Prefers a warm and sunny spot.
Pruning: Optional or hard.

HIGHLIGHTS
This is an excellent clematis to add to your collection. For its
sheer uniqueness it cannot be matched. It produces masses
of perfectly-shaped incandescent flowers that are spellbinding.
It makes a good choice for a tall trellis.

ANECDOTAL
Francisque Morel of Lyon, France, raised 'Huldine' circa 1914.
He gave the seedling to William Robinson of Gravetye Manor.
Mr. Robinson's head gardener, Ernest Markham,
subsequently introduced it to the clematis
gardening world in 1934.

C. 'Huldine'

FLOWER FEATURES AND PLANT CHARACTERISTICS
The tepal's upper side resembles Mother of Pearl. The backside
is pale mauve with a dark center bar. The flower is 2" to 4"
in diameter with 6 slightly bowed tepals.
Its stamens are creamy-yellow.

Clematis integrifolia
(common name: Bush Clematis)

PRONUNCIATION
in-teg-gri-<u>fo</u>-lee-ah

HERITAGE
Country of Origin: Southern Europe

GROWING ZONES
USDA Growing Zones 4 thru 11.

BLOOMING PERIOD
In USDA Zones 4 thru 9 later in the season and may repeat.
In USDA Zones 10 & 11 later in the season and repeats.

Height Range: One to two and a half feet.
Light Exposure: It thrives equally in sunny or shady locations.
Pruning: Hard. It will die to the ground in the colder zones.

HIGHLIGHTS
Clematis integrifolia is a non-climbing plant. These sweet
nodding bells make it an excellent choice to place in the
front of a mixed border. Its compact size makes it
perfect for a container.

ANECDOTAL
Introduced to Great Britian in 1573, it is the parent
plant of many clematis cultivars.

C. integrifolia

FLOWER FEATURES AND PLANT CHARACTERISTICS

The flower's tepals are a deep violet-blue and form a bell-shaped
flower. The flower is 1½" to 2" in diameter with 4 deeply
ribbed tepals. Its stamens are yellow.

Clematis 'Jackmanii'

{1863}

Pronunciation
Jack-<u>man</u>-ee-eye

Heritage
Hybridizer: George Jackman & Son
Country of Origin: United Kingdom
Parentage: *C.* 'Atrorubens' x *C. lanuginosa*

Growing Zones
USDA Growing Zones 4 thru 11.

Blooming Period
In USDA Zones 4 thru 9 later in the season and may repeat.
In USDA Zones 10 & 11 later in the season and repeats.

Height Range: Eight to twelve feet (sometimes taller).
Light Exposure: It thrives equally in sunny or shady locations.
Pruning: Optional or hard.

Highlights
Grow this timeless classic for its masses of attractive purple
blossoms and dependable performance. It will easily
scale a tall trellis.

Anecdotal
'Jackmanii' it still as sought-after today as when it was first
introduced. Raised in 1858, this was the first of many clematis
attributed to Mr. Jackman. It is considered by some to be the most
popular in the world. It is the parent responsible for countless
crosses of many favorite cultivars we know today such as
'Victoria', 'Gipsy Queen', and 'The President'.

C. 'Jackmanii'

FLOWER FEATURES AND PLANT CHARACTERISTICS

The flower's tepals are colored a deep velvety-purple. The flower is 4" to 6" in diameter and usually has 4 large tepals but at times can produce 5 or 6. Its stamens are greenish-beige.

Clematis 'Jackmanii Alba'

{1878}

PRONUNCIATION
Jack-<u>man</u>-ee-eye

HERITAGE
Hybridizer: Charles Noble
Country of Origin: United Kingdom
Parentage: *C.* 'Fortunei' x *C.* 'Jackmanii'

GROWING ZONES
USDA Growing Zones 4 thru 11.

BLOOMING PERIOD
In USDA Zones 4 thru 9 later in the season and may repeat.
In USDA Zones 10 & 11 later in the season and repeats.

Height Range: Eight to twelve feet.
Light Exposure: It thrives equally in sunny
or shady locations.
Pruning: Optional or hard.

HIGHLIGHTS
Grow this clematis for its delightful coloring.
It blooms freely and consistently. Combine it with
Clematis 'Jackmanii' for an unforgettable combination.
It can produce double flowers in
USDA Zones 4 through 9.

C. 'Jackmanii Alba'

FLOWER FEATURES AND PLANT CHARACTERISTICS

The flower's tepals are colored an elegant white with a bluish-mauve tint. The flower is 4" to 6" in diameter and has 5 to 6 and at times more twisted tepals. Its stamens are beige.

Clematis 'Josephine'

(syn. *C.* 'Evijohill')

{1998}

HERITAGE
Discoverer: Josephine Hill
Country of Origin: United Kingdom
Parentage: Unknown

GROWING ZONES
USDA Growing Zones 4 thru 11.

BLOOMING PERIOD
Early in the season and repeats.

Height Range: Six to eight feet.
Light Exposure: In hotter locales it is best planted in an area
with some shade to prevent the flowers from fading.
Pruning: Optional or light.

HIGHLIGHTS
Eye-catching to say the least, 'Josephine' is a new clematis
introduction with a very distinctive look. It puts on quite a
show. Early season blooms located in more shaded areas
will have a green tinge to them.

ANECDOTAL
This English introduction was discovered by Mrs. Josephine
Hill sometime in the 1980's. Raymond Evison introduced
it at the Chelsea Flower Show in 1998.

C. 'Josephine'

FLOWER FEATURES AND PLANT CHARACTERISTICS
The flower's tepals form attractive double dahlia-like flower that are colored a mauvish-pink with darker striping. The flower is 3" to 5" in diameter. Its stamens are not visible.

Clematis 'Kathleen Dunford'

{1962}

PRONUNCIATION
<u>Dun</u>-ford

HERITAGE
Discoverer: Kathleen Dunford
Country of Origin: United Kingdom
Parentage: Unknown

GROWING ZONES
USDA Growing Zones 4 thru 11.

BLOOMING PERIOD
Early in the season and repeats.

Height Range: Six to eight feet.
Light Exposure: It thrives equally in sunny
or shady locations.
Pruning: Optional or light.

HIGHLIGHTS
This is an intriguing clematis because of its coloring
which is accentuated by contrasting stamens. It makes
a good container selection.

ANECDOTAL
Raised in the garden of Miss Kathleen Dunford around
1950, it was later introduced by Jim Fisk.

C. 'Kathleen Dunford'

FLOWER FEATURES AND PLANT CHARACTERISTICS
The flower's tepals are colored a speckled, deep rosy-purple.
In USDA Zones 4 to 9, early flowers are semi-double
and consist of two overlapping layers of tepals. Fall flowers
are single. In USDA Zones 10 & 11, they are only single.
The flower is 7" to 9" in diameter and has 6 to 8 tepals
that are very pointed. Its stamens are red.

Clematis 'Ken Donson'

HERITAGE
Hybridizer: Walter Pennell
Country of Origin: United Kingdom
Parentage: *C.* 'Daniel Deronda' x *C.* 'Barbara Jackman'

GROWING ZONES
USDA Growing Zones 4 thru 11.

BLOOMING PERIOD
Early in the season and repeats.

Height Range: Six to eight feet.
Light Exposure: It thrives equally in sunny
or shady locations.
Pruning: Optional or light.

HIGHLIGHTS
This striking cultivar is much admired for its large
tepals. It would attractively adorn a
medium-sized obelisk.

ANECDOTAL
In 1976, Mr. Pennell named this clematis after his
long-time devoted employee, Ken Donson.

C. 'Ken Donson'

FLOWER FEATURES AND PLANT CHARACTERISTICS
The flower's tepals are an appealing deep lavender-blue.
The flower is 6" to 7" in diameter and has 6 very large tepals.
Its stamens are golden.

Clematis 'King Edward VII'

Hybridizer: George Jackman & Son
Country of Origin: United Kingdom
Parentage: *C.* 'Fairy Queen' x *C. texensis* 'Sir Trevor Lawrence'

GROWING ZONES
USDA Growing Zones 4 thru 11.

BLOOMING PERIOD
Early in the season and repeats.

Height Range: Up to six feet.
Light Exposure: It thrives equally in sunny
or shady locations.
Pruning: Optional or light.

HIGHLIGHTS
This regal clematis is a perfect choice for a container
because of its compact size. You will love it for its paisley
coloring and repeat performances.

ANECDOTAL
George Jackman raised this clematis in about 1902.
He used a very interesting combination
for its parentage.

C. 'King Edward VII'

FLOWER FEATURES AND PLANT CHARACTERISTICS
The flower's tepals are speckled an attractive lilac-mauve.
The flower is 6" to 8" in diameter and has
6 to 8 overlapping tepals.
Its stamens are beige.

Clematis 'Lady Betty Balfour'

{1912}

PRONUNCIATION
Ball-4

HERITAGE
Hybridizer: George Jackman & Son
Country of Origin: United Kingdom
Parentage: *C.* 'Gipsy Queen' x *C.* 'Beauty of Worcester'

GROWING ZONES
USDA Growing Zones 4 thru 11.

BLOOMING PERIOD
Later in the season.

Height Range: Eight to twelve feet.
Light Exposure: It does best when planted in full sun.
Pruning: Optional or hard.

HIGHLIGHTS
This is a clematis that is grown for is continuous display
of late summer blooms. A warm and sunny location is a
must. It is trouble-free and vigorous and an excellent
choice for a pergola or an arbor.

ANECDOTAL
Named after a patron of Jackman & Son's nursery in
Woking, England, Lady Betty Balfour had a fine garden
close by which was created with the assistance of
the famous horticulturist, Gertrude Jekyll.

C. 'Lady Betty Balfour'

FLOWER FEATURES AND PLANT CHARACTERISTICS

The flower's tepals are colored a deep violet-blue with a hint of red near the base. The flower is 6" to 8" in diameter and has 6 wide and over-lapping tepals. Its stamens are a contrasting yellow.

Clematis 'Lady Northcliffe'

(syn. *C.* 'Lady Northcliff')

{1906}

PRONUNCIATION
Lady <u>North</u>-cliff

HERITAGE
Hybridizer: George Jackman & Son
Country of Origin: United Kingdom
Parentage: *C.* 'Beauty of Worcester' x *C.* 'Otto Fröebel'

GROWING ZONES
USDA Growing Zones 4 thru 11.

BLOOMING PERIOD
Early in the season and repeats.

Height Range: Up to six feet.
Light Exposure: It thrives equally in sunny
or shady locations.
Pruning: Optional or light.

HIGHLIGHTS
A clematis of rare simple beauty, this is a long time favorite
because of its free-flowering ability. It is a perfect selection
for a container or small trellis.

C. 'Lady Northcliffe'

FLOWER FEATURES AND PLANT CHARACTERISTICS
The flower's tepals are colored a rich lavender-blue. The
flower is 4" to 6" in diameter and has 6 overlapping
wavy-edged tepals. Its stamens are colored ivory,
producing a pleasing contrast.

Clematis lanuginosa 'Candida'

(syn. *C.* 'Candida')

{1862}

PRONUNCIATION
la-<u>new</u>-gin-no-sah Can-<u>dee</u>-dah

HERITAGE
Hybridizer: Victor Lemoine & Sons
Country of Origin: France
Parentage: *C. lanuginosa* x *C. patens*

GROWING ZONES
USDA Growing Zones 4 thru 11.

BLOOMING PERIOD
Early in the season and repeats.

Height Range: Six to eight feet.
Light Exposure: It thrives equally in sunny
or shady locations.
Pruning: Optional or light.

HIGHLIGHTS
High marks are given for it luxurious white
coloring and repeat performance.

C. lanuginosa 'Candida'

FLOWER FEATURES AND PLANT CHARACTERISTICS
The flower's tepals are a dazzling pure-white. The flower
is 6" to 8" in diameter and has 6 to 8 very wide
overlapping tepals. Its stamens are pale yellow.

Clematis 'Lasurstern'

{1905}

PRONUNCIATION
Laz-ur-stern

HERITAGE
Hybridizer: Goos & Koenemann
Country of Origin: Germany
Parentage: Unknown

GROWING ZONES
USDA Growing Zones 4 thru 11.

BLOOMING PERIOD
Early in the season and repeats.

Height Range: Six to nine feet.
Light Exposure: It thrives equally in sunny
or shady locations.
Pruning: Optional or light.

HIGHLIGHTS
Its stellar good looks are created by its exquisitely
formed flowers and its contrasting colored stamens.
This time-honored classic does well on
a wall or trellis.

ANECDOTAL
Lasurstern is German for "Azure Star". In
USDA Zones 4 to 9, it may occasionally produce
semi-double flowers. Looks wonderful
in the sun or shade.

C. 'Lasurstern'

FLOWER FEATURES AND PLANT CHARACTERISTICS

The flower's tepals are a luxuriously lavender-blue. The flower is 7" to 8" in diameter and has 6 to 8 very large overlapping tepals. Its stamens are yellow.

Clematis 'Lincoln Star'

{1954}

HERITAGE
Hybridizer: Walter Pennell
Country of Origin: United Kingdom
Parentage: A seedling of *C.* 'Nelly Moser'

GROWING ZONES
USDA Growing Zones 4 thru 11.

BLOOMING PERIOD
Early in the season and repeats.

Height Range: Six to eight feet.
Light Exposure: It is best planted in an area with some
shade to prevent the flowers from fading.
Pruning: Optional or light.

HIGHLIGHTS
The star-like blossoms of this clematis are painted with
pretty stripes. More compact than its parent 'Nelly Moser',
it makes a great choice for a container.

ANECDOTAL
It exhibits many similarities to the parent seedling.

C. 'Lincoln Star'

FLOWER FEATURES AND PLANT CHARACTERISTICS
The flower's tepals are colored a lively raspberry-pink in the
center margins while the edges are a paler pink. The flower
is 6" to 8" in diameter and has 8 pointed tepals.
Its stamens are maroon.

Clematis 'Lord Nevill'

(syn. *C.* 'Lord Neville')

{1878}

PRONUNCIATION
(rhymes with devil)

HERITAGE
Hybridizer: Thomas Cripps & Son
Country of Origin: United Kingdom
Parentage: *C. patens* x *C.* 'Standishii'

GROWING ZONES
USDA Growing Zones 4 thru 11.

BLOOMING PERIOD
Early in the season and repeats.

Height Range: Six to eight feet.
Light Exposure: It thrives equally in sunny
or shady locations.
Pruning: Optional or light.

HIGHLIGHTS
This refined and elegant clematis is a long-time favorite.
Its flowers are long-lasting and it is perfectly suited for
a container because of its compact size.

ANECDOTAL
Thomas Cripps & Son named it after Lord Nevill of
Tunbridge Wells, who may have been one
of their patrons.

C. 'Lord Nevill'

FLOWER FEATURES AND PLANT CHARACTERISTICS
The flower's tepals are colored a rich, deep violet-blue
with pretty ruffled edges. The flower is 6" to 8" in diameter
and has 6 to 8 tepals. Its stamens are purple.

Clematis 'Louise Rowe'

{1983}

PRONUNCIATION
Row

HERITAGE
Hybridizer: Mrs. Jean B. Rowe
Country of Origin: United Kingdom
Parentage: *C.* 'Marie Boisselot' x *C.* 'William Kennett'

GROWING ZONES
USDA Growing Zones 4 thru 11.

BLOOMING PERIOD
Early in the season and repeats.

Height Range: Four to six feet.
Light Exposure: In hotter locales it is best planted in an area
with some shade to prevent the flowers from fading.
Pruning: Optional or light.

HIGHLIGHTS
This is one of the prettiest clematis because of its
pleasing shape and alluring coloring. It makes an excellent
container selection. A perfect combination when paired
with *Clematis* 'William Kennett'.

ANECDOTAL
Raised by Mrs. Rowe and introduced by Jim Fisk.

C. 'Louise Rowe'
FLOWER FEATURES AND PLANT CHARACTERISTICS
The tepals are colored a delicate lilac-mauve that gradually fades
to white. In USDA Zones 4 to 9, early flowers can bloom double,
semi-double and single simultaneously on the same plant. Fall
flowers are single. In USDA Zones 10 & 11, flowers are *only* single.
The flower is 4" to 6" in diameter with rounded tepals.
Its stamens are creamy-yellow.

Clematis 'Madame Baron-Veillard'

(syn. *C.* 'Mme Baron-Veillard' or *C.* 'Madame Baron Veillard')

{1885}

PRONUNCIATION
Mah-dahm or Ma-dom Ba-row-vay-yar

HERITAGE
Hybridizer: Baron-Veillard
Country of Origin: France
Parentage: Unknown

GROWING ZONES
USDA Growing Zones 4 thru 11.

BLOOMING PERIOD
In USDA Zones 4 thru 9 later in the season and may repeat.
In USDA Zones 10 & 11 later in the season and repeats.

Height Range: Eight to twelve feet.
Light Exposure: It performs best when planted in full sun.
Pruning: Optional or hard.

HIGHLIGHTS
Take advantage of its height by growing it on an arbor or
pergola with another tall clematis or climbing rose. It is very
vigorous and free-flowering, preferring a warm sunny place. It
is a popular clematis because of its prolific blooming
ability and the flower's longevity.

ANECDOTAL
Believed to be named after the wife of the breeder, the
correct spelling of the last name has a hyphen.

C. 'Madame Baron-Veillard'

FLOWER FEATURES AND PLANT CHARACTERISTICS

The flower's tepals are colored a velvety lilac-pink. The flower is 4" to 6" to in diameter and has 6 tepals that curve back slightly. Its stamens are creamy-white.

Clematis 'Madame Grangé'

{1873}

PRONUNCIATION
Mah-dahm or Ma-dom Grahn-jay

HERITAGE
Hybridizer: M. Théophile Grangé
Country of Origin: France
Parentage: *C. lanuginosa* x *C.* 'Ruba Grandiflora'

GROWING ZONES
USDA Growing Zones 4 thru 11.

BLOOMING PERIOD
In USDA Zones 4 thru 11 later in the season and may repeat.
In USDA Zones 10 & 11 later in the season and may repeat.

Height Range: Eight to twelve feet.
Light Exposure: It thrives equally in sunny
or shady locations.
Pruning: Optional or hard.

HIGHLIGHTS
Grow this clematis for it luxurious flowers and uniquely
shaped tepals. It is a vigorous and trouble-free clematis that
can easily scale a tall trellis.

C. 'Madame Grangé'

Flower Features and Plant Characteristics

The flower's tepals are a breathtaking velvety carmine when it first opens and as it ages it turns a dusky purple. The flower is 4" to 6" in diameter and has 4 to 6 boat-shaped tepals that curl upward revealing a silvery underside.

It stamens are dark beige.

Clematis 'Margaret Hunt'

{1969}

HERITAGE
Hybridizer: Margaret Hunt
Country of Origin: United Kingdom
Parentage: Unknown

GROWING ZONES
USDA Growing Zones 4 thru 11.

BLOOMING PERIOD
In USDA Zones 4 thru 9 later in the season and may repeat.
In USDA Zones 10 & 11 later in the season and repeats.

Height Range: Eight to ten feet.
Light Exposure: It thrives equally in sunny
or shady locations.
Pruning: Optional or hard.

HIGHLIGHTS
Petite but prolific, it delivers delightful clouds of small pink
flowers with nicely colored stamens. Another nice tall pink
variety, this clematis is well suited to grow on a tall trellis.

ANECDOTAL
In the early 1960's Margaret Hunt, a gardener in Norfolk,
England, raised this clematis which was later
introduced by Jim Fisk.

C. 'Margaret Hunt'

FLOWER FEATURES AND PLANT CHARACTERISTICS
The flower's tepals are colored a dusky mauve-pink. The flower
is 4" to 6" in diameter and has 6 petite star-shaped tepals
that taper to a point. It stamens are coffee-colored.

Clematis 'Marie Boisselot'

{1890}

PRONUNCIATION
Marie Bwass-<u>low</u>

HERITAGE
Hybridizer: Auguste Boisselot
Country of Origin: France
Parentage: Unknown

GROWING ZONES
USDA Growing Zones 4 thru 11.

BLOOMING PERIOD
Early in the season and repeats.

Height Range: Six to ten feet.
Light Exposure: It thrives equally in sunny
or shady locations.
Pruning: Optional or light.

HIGHLIGHTS
The sheer elegance of this exquisite French introduction
makes it a must for any garden. The tepals are a large,
luminescent white, reminiscent of the moon.
Perfect for an obelisk.

ANECDOTAL
Considered one of the best of the white clematis.

C. 'Marie Boisselot'

FLOWER FEATURES AND PLANT CHARACTERISTICS
The flower's tepals are colored a brilliant pure-white. The flower is 6" to 8" in diameter and has 8 very wide tepals. Its stamens are pale yellow.

Clematis 'Masquerade'

{1993}

PRONUNCIATION
Mass-ker-<u>aid</u>

HERITAGE
Hybridizer: Unknown
Country of Origin: United Kingdom
Parentage: Unknown

GROWING ZONES
USDA Growing Zones 4 thru 11.

BLOOMING PERIOD
Early in the season and repeats.

Height Range: Up to six feet.
Light Exposure: It thrives equally in sunny
or shady locations.
Pruning: Optional or light.

HIGHLIGHTS
This clematis does not have to hide its beauty behind a
mask. Each blossom consists of a magical color combination.
This relatively short plant makes an excellent
candidate for a container.

ANECDOTAL
Introduced by Raymond Evison.

C. 'Masquerade'

FLOWER FEATURES AND PLANT CHARACTERISTICS
The flower's tepals are colored a gorgeous pale-lavender with a darker center bar. The flower is 6" to 8" in diameter and has 6 wavy-edged tepals. It stamens are wine red.

Clematis 'Miss Bateman'

{1869}

PRONUNCIATION
Miss <u>Bait</u>-man

HERITAGE
Hybridizer: Charles Noble
Country of Origin: United Kingdom
Parentage: *C.* 'Fortunei' x *C.* 'Standishii'

GROWING ZONES
USDA Growing Zones 4 thru 11.

BLOOMING PERIOD
Early in the season and repeats.

Height Range: Six to eight feet.
Light Exposure: It thrives equally in sunny
or shady locations.
Pruning: Optional or light.

HIGHLIGHTS
Simple and elegant, it is loved for its unique coloring. Its
early flowers are often colored green and later ones initially have
green central stripes. With its compact size it is an
excellent container selection. If you prefer the green
bars, planting it in the shade will extend
the length of time this trait occurs.

ANECDOTAL
It is named after Catherine Bateman, the daughter of
James Bateman, a renowned orchid grower and builder of the
famous gardens at Biddulph Grange in the United Kingdom.

C. 'Miss Bateman'

FLOWER FEATURES AND PLANT CHARACTERISTICS
The flower's tepals are colored a pretty creamy-white.
The flower is 4" to 6" in diameter and has 8 tepals.
Its stamens are reddish-brown.

Clematis 'Mrs. Cholmondeley'

{circa 1873}

PRONUNCIATION
Mrs. Chumley

HERITAGE
Hybridizer: Charles Noble
Country of Origin: United Kingdom
Parentage: *C.* 'Fortunei' x *C.* 'Jackmanii'

GROWING ZONES
USDA Growing Zones 4 thru 11.

BLOOMING PERIOD
Early in the season and repeats.

Height Range: Six to ten feet.
Light Exposure: It thrives equally in sunny
or shady locations.
Pruning: Optional or light.

HIGHLIGHTS
This is a wonderful time-honored cultivar. It gets high
marks for being a nice repeat bloomer. Great for
small gardens or on an obelisk.

C. 'Mrs. Cholmondeley'

FLOWER FEATURES AND PLANT CHARACTERISTICS
The flower's tepals are an attractive pale lavender-blue. The flower is 6" to 8" in diameter and has 6 to 8 uniquely spaced tepals. Its stamens are beige colored.

Clematis 'Mrs. George Jackman'

{1875}

HERITAGE
Hybridizer: George Jackman & Son
Country of Origin: United Kingdom
Parentage: *C. lanuginosa* 'Candida' x *C.* 'Fortunei'

GROWING ZONES
USDA Growing Zones 4 thru 11.

BLOOMING PERIOD
Early in the season and repeats.

Height Range: Six to eight feet.
Light Exposure: It thrives equally in sunny
or shady locations.
Pruning: Optional or light.

HIGHLIGHTS
This charming and easy-to-grow clematis provides
a nice show of attractive medium-sized flowers.
Long-lasting blooms make it sensational in
floral arrangements or bouquets.

C. 'Mrs. George Jackman'

FLOWER FEATURES AND PLANT CHARACTERISTICS

The flower's tepals are colored a beautiful ivory-white. In
USDA Zones 4 thru 9 early flowers are semi-double and
late season flowers are single. Flowers are *only* single in
USDA Zones 10 & 11. The flower is 5" to 7"
in diameter and has 6 to 8 rounded tepals.
Its stamens are pinkish-beige.

Clematis 'Mrs. N. Thompson'

{1961}

HERITAGE
Hybridizer: Walter Pennell
Country of Origin: United Kingdom
Parentage: Unknown

GROWING ZONES
USDA Growing Zones 4 thru 11.

BLOOMING PERIOD
Early in the season and repeats.

Height Range: Five to seven feet.
Light Exposure: It thrives equally in sunny
or shady locations.
Pruning: Optional or light.

HIGHLIGHTS
This clematis is grown for its vivid eye-catching colors.
It makes an excellent container selection
because of it short stature.

ANECDOTAL
Named after the wife of Mr. N. Thompson, who
was Pennell's nursery office manager in 1954.

C. 'Mrs. N. Thompson'

<small>FLOWER FEATURES AND PLANT CHARACTERISTICS</small>
The flower's tepals are colored a dramatic, deep violet-blue
and has an intense scarlet red bar. The flower is 4" to 6" in
diameter and has 4, 5, or 6 tepals that are overlapping.
Its stamens are reddish.

Clematis 'Mrs. P. B. Truax'

PRONUNCIATION
True-ax

HERITAGE
Hybridizer: George Jackman & Son
Country of Origin: United Kingdom
Parentage: Unknown

GROWING ZONES
USDA Growing Zones 4 thru 11.

BLOOMING PERIOD
Early in the season and repeats.

Height Range: Six to ten feet.
Light Exposure: It thrives equally in sunny
or shady locations.
Pruning: Optional or light.

HIGHLIGHTS
This charming clematis is beautifully colored and
is moderately vigorous. A lovely clematis to combine
with a yellow rose.

C. 'Mrs. P. B. Truax'

FLOWER FEATURES AND PLANT CHARACTERISTICS

The flower's tepals are colored a silky periwinkle-blue. The flower is 4" to 6" in diameter and has 8 tepals that taper narrowly towards the base. Its stamens are creamy-yellow.

Clematis 'Mrs. Spencer Castle'

{circa 1924}

HERITAGE
Hybridizer: George Jackman & Son
Country of Origin: United Kingdom
Parentage: Unknown

GROWING ZONES
USDA Growing Zones 4 thru 11.

BLOOMING PERIOD
Early in the season and repeats.

Height Range: Six to eight feet.
Light Exposure: It thrives equally in sunny
or shady locations.
Pruning: Optional or light.

HIGHLIGHTS
The soft strawberry ice cream coloring would look
fabulous combined with a dark red or burgundy
clematis. Excellent candidate for a container
or short trellis.

C. 'Mrs. Spencer Castle'

FLOWER FEATURES AND PLANT CHARACTERISTICS
The flower's tepals are colored a unique mauve-pink color.
Early flowers are both semi-double and single and fall flowers
are single in USDA Zones 4 to 9 but are *only* single in
USDA Zones 10 & 11. The flower is 4" to 6" in diameter.
It stamens are yellow.

Clematis 'Multi Blue'

(syn. *C.* 'Multiblue' or *C.* 'Multi-blue')

{1983}

HERITAGE
Hybridizer: J. Bouter & Zoon
Country of Origin: Holland
Parentage: A sport of *C.* 'The President'

GROWING ZONES
USDA Growing Zones 4 thru 11.

BLOOMING PERIOD
Early in the season and repeats.

Height Range: Six to eight feet.
Light Exposure: It thrives equally in sunny
or shady locations.
Pruning: Optional or light.

HIGHLIGHTS
A captivating clematis that never disappoints. After
the outer tepals fall off, the inner pointed rosette remains
on the plant for a long time enhancing its longevity.
Can been grow in containers.

C. 'Multi Blue'

<small>FLOWER FEATURES AND PLANT CHARACTERISTICS</small>
The flower's tepals create a unique double flower. They are colored a lavender-blue. The flowers are 4" to 5" in diameter and form a neat dome-shaped rosette. Its stamens are not visible.

Clematis 'Nelly Moser'

(syn. *C.* 'Nellie Moser')

{1897}

PRONUNCIATION
Mo-zur

HERITAGE
Hybridizer: Frances Moser
Country of Origin: France
Parentage: *C.* 'Bélisaire' x *C.* 'Marcel Moser'

GROWING ZONES
USDA Growing Zones 4 thru 11.

BLOOMING PERIOD
Early in the season and repeats.

Height Range: Six to ten feet.
Light Exposure: It is best planted in an area with some
shade to prevent the flowers from fading.
Pruning: Optional or light.

HIGHLIGHTS
This charming and easy to grow French clematis is popular
because of its prolific blooming ability and vigor. A good
choice to grow on a trellis in the shade.

ANECDOTAL
Behind 'Jackmanii', it is probably the second best known
clematis cultivar and is often the striped clematis by
which others are judged.

C. 'Nelly Moser'

FLOWER FEATURES AND PLANT CHARACTERISTICS

The flower's tepals are colored a subtle mauve-pink with a deep
carmine bar. The color intensity and width of the central bar can
change with each season. The flower is 7" to 9" in diameter
and has 8 overlapping tepals. The stamens are maroon.

Clematis 'Niobe'

{1975}

PRONUNCIATION
Nigh-<u>oh</u>-bee

HERITAGE
Hybridizer: Wladyslaw Noll
Country of Origin: Poland
Parentage: Unknown

GROWING ZONES
USDA Growing Zones 4 thru 11.

BLOOMING PERIOD
Early in the season and repeats.

Height Range: Four to six feet.
Light Exposure: It will grow in any location but it
performs best in a sunny location.
Pruning: Optional or hard.

HIGHLIGHTS
Consistently popular with gardeners, it is considered to be
one of the best red clematis because of it incredible coloring.
Due to its compact nature, it is a great container cultivar.

ANECDOTAL
In Greek mythology, Niobe's seven sons and seven daughters
were slain by the gods. In her grief she was unable to stop
weeping. The gods, taking pity on her, decided to end her
misery by turning her into stone.

C. 'Niobe'

FLOWER FEATURES AND PLANT CHARACTERISTICS

The flower's tepals are colored a velvety, deep ruby-red but as they emerge they are nearly black. The flower is 4" to 6" in diameter and has 6 tepals. Its stamens are light yellow.

Clematis 'Otto Fröebel'

(syn. *C.* 'Otto Froebel')

{1871}

PRONUNCIATION
Oh-toe Fruh-bull

HERITAGE
Hybridizer: Victor Lemoine and Sons
Country of Origin: France
Parentage: *C. patens* x *C. lanuginosa*

GROWING ZONES
USDA Growing Zones 4 thru 11.

BLOOMING PERIOD
Early in the season and repeats.

Height Range: Six to eight feet.
Light Exposure: It is best planted in an area with
some shade to prevent the flowers from fading.
Pruning: Optional or light.

HIGHLIGHTS
A tried and true French cultivar that has classic good looks.
An excellent choice for a container.

ANECDOTAL
At one time thought to be lost, this clematis was recently
reintroduced. It was named in honor of Mr. Fröebel, who
was a well-known Swiss nurseryman of his generation.

C. 'Otto Fröbel'

FLOWER FEATURES AND PLANT CHARACTERISTICS
The flower's tepals emerge pale mauve turning to a
stunning antique-white. The flower is 6" to 8"
in diameter and has 8 wavy tepals.
Its stamens are reddish-brown.

Clematis 'Perle d'Azur'

{1885}

PRONUNCIATION
Pearl dah <u>Sure</u>

HERITAGE
Hybridizer: Frances (Francisque) Morel
Country of Origin: France
Parentage: *C. lanuginosa caerulea* x *C. viticella* 'Modesta'

GROWING ZONES
USDA Growing Zones 4 thru 11.

BLOOMING PERIOD
In USDA Zones 4 thru 9 later in the season and may repeat.
In USDA Zones 10 & 11 late in the season and repeats.

Height Range: Six to ten (possibly taller) feet.
Light Exposure: It thrives equally in sunny
or shady locations.
Pruning: Optional or hard.

HIGHLIGHTS
This clematis is a venerable classic climber. Pair it with a
shorter clematis because its lowers stems are free of foliage.

ANECDOTAL
The translation of 'Perle d'Azur' is "Azure Pearl". In
England there is a stunning specimen of 'Perle d'Azur'
growing in the garden at Sissinghurst castle.

C. 'Perle d'Azur'

<small>Flower Features and Plant Characteristics</small>
The flower's tepals are colored a clear, mid-violet blue.
The flower is 4" to 6" in diameter and has 4 to 6
semi-nodding tepals with deeply channeled midribs.
Its stamens are greenish-yellow.

Clematis 'Perrin's Pride'

PRONUNCIATION
Per-rinz

HERITAGE
Hybridizer: Arthur H. Steffen
Country of Origin: U.S.A
Parentage: Unknown

GROWING ZONES
USDA Growing Zones 4 thru 11.

BLOOMING PERIOD
In USDA Zones 4 thru 9 later in the season and may repeat.
In USDA Zones 10 & 11 early in the season and repeats.

Height Range: Six to eight feet.
Light Exposure: It thrives equally in sunny
or shady locations.
Pruning: Optional or hard.

HIGHLIGHTS
This free-flowering charmer is easy to grow and is
considered to be one of the best American cultivars.
Excellent choice for a container.

ANECDOTAL
This is the Steffen's nursery's first large hybrid
clematis thought to be introduced in 1987.

C. 'Perrin's Pride'
FLOWER FEATURES AND PLANT CHARACTERISTICS
The flower's tepals are colored a splendid deep-purple. The
flower is 5" in diameter and has 4 to 6 overlapping tepals.
It stamens are yellow.

Clematis 'Petit Faucon'

{1995}

PRONUNCIATION
Puh-<u>tee</u> Fo-<u>co</u>

HERITAGE
Hybridizer: Raymond Evison
Country of Origin: United Kingdom
Parentage: A seedling of *C.* 'Daniel Deronda' that was most likely
crossed with *C. integrifolia* or *C. diversifolia.*

GROWING ZONES
USDA Growing Zones 4 thru 11.

BLOOMING PERIOD
Late in the season and may repeat.

Height Range: Up to 3 feet.
Light Exposure: It thrives equally in sunny
or shady locations.
Pruning: Hard. It will die to the ground
in the colder zones.

HIGHLIGHTS
This attractive new introduction is best suited
as a border plant. It is an herbaceous,
non-climbing clematis.

ANECDOTAL
The name 'Petit Faucon' is French for
"little falcon".

C. 'Petit Faucon'

FLOWER FEATURES AND PLANT CHARACTERISTICS

The flower's tepals are colored an intense deep-purple and form a nodding bell. The flower is 2½" to 3½" in diameter and has 4 to 6 twisting tepals. Its stamens are yellow.

Clematis 'Peveril Pearl'

{1979}

PRONUNCIATION
Pev-er-<u>eel</u> Pearl

HERITAGE
Hybridizer: Barry Fretwell
Country of Origin: United Kingdom
Parentage: Unknown

GROWING ZONES
USDA Growing Zones 4 thru 11.

BLOOMING PERIOD
Early in the season and repeats.

Height Range: Six to eight feet.
Light Exposure: It is best planted in an area with
some shade to prevent the flowers from fading.
Pruning: Optional or light.

HIGHLIGHTS
Just like a pearl, its iridescent coloring dazzles in the shade.
The fact that the flowers are so large makes it even more
impressive. A great container plant.

C. 'Peveril Pearl'

FLOWER FEATURES AND PLANT CHARACTERISTICS
The flower's tepals are colored a delicate lilac-pink and are
graced with a pink bar. The flower is 8" in diameter and
has 6 to 8 tepals. Its stamens are pinkish-brown.

Clematis 'Piilu'

{2000}

PRONUNCIATION
<u>Pie</u>-loo

HERITAGE
Hybridizer: Uno and Ali Kivistik
Country of Origin: Estonia (U.S.S.R.)
Parentage: *C.* 'Hagley Hybrid' x *C.* 'Makhrovyi'

GROWING ZONES
USDA Growing Zones 4 thru 11.

BLOOMING PERIOD
Early to mid season and repeats.

Height Range: Four to six feet.
Light Exposure: It thrives equally in sunny
or shady locations.
Pruning: Optional or hard.

HIGHLIGHTS
This splendid new introduction is neatly compact,
making it an excellent container candidate.

ANECDOTAL
The name 'Piilu' is Estonian for "little duckling".
The Kivisik family is actively involved in breeding
clematis and have produced an impressive 140
new cultivars and counting.

C. 'Piilu'

FLOWER FEATURES AND PLANT CHARACTERISTICS

The flower's tepals are colored a charming pastel-pink with a stunning raspberry bar. In USDA Zones 4 thru 9 the early flowers are double and late season flowers are single. Only single flowers are produced in USDA Zones 10 & 11. The flower is 4" to 5" in diameter and has 4 to 6 crenulated tepals.
It stamens are golden-yellow.

Clematis 'Pink Champagne'

(syn. *C.* 'Kakio')

{circa 1980}

HERITAGE
Hybridizer: Kazushige Ozawa
Country of Origin: Japan
Parentage: Possibly *C.* 'Star of India' x *C.* 'Ernest Markham'.

GROWING ZONES
USDA Growing Zones 4 thru 11.

BLOOMING PERIOD
Early in the season and repeats.

HEIGHT RANGE: SIX TO EIGHT FEET.
Light Exposure: Plant in any location but in very hot areas it is
best planted in some shade to prevent the flowers from fading.
Pruning: Optional or light.

HIGHLIGHTS
Greatly admired for its captivating coloring, it is an excellent
free-flowering variety. Because of its compact size, it is
ideal for containers or a small shade garden.

ANECDOTAL
This stunning clematis was raised by Mr. Ozawa in
1971. Originally naming it 'Kakio', he later changed
the name to 'Pink Champagne' to gain the attention of
the western market. Kakio is a region in Japan.

C. 'Pink Champagne'

FLOWER FEATURES AND PLANT CHARACTERISTICS
The flower's tepals are colored an intense mauve-pink
with a delicate pink central bar. The flower is 6" to 8"
in diameter and has 6 to 8 overlapping tepals.
Its stamens are a contrasting yellow.

Clematis 'Prince Charles'

{1976}

HERITAGE
Hybridizer: Alister Keay
Country of Origin: New Zealand
Parentage: Unknown

GROWING ZONES
USDA Growing Zones 4 thru 11.

BLOOMING PERIOD
In USDA Zones 4 thru 9 later in the season and may repeat.
In USDA Zones 10 & 11 early in the season and repeats.

Height Range: Up to six feet.
Light Exposure: It thrives equally in sunny
or shady locations.
Pruning: Optional or hard.

HIGHLIGHTS
Producing masses of medium-sized blooms, this compact
variety is a perfect clematis to combine with taller hybrids
whose barren lower stems need camouflaging.
Free-flowering and easy to grow.

ANECDOTAL
Named after H.R.H. Prince Charles.

C. 'Prince Charles'

FLOWER FEATURES AND PLANT CHARACTERISTICS
The flower's tepals are colored a bluish-mauve. The flower is
4" in diameter and has 4 to 6 medium-sized tepals with midribs.
Its stamens are greenish-yellow.

Clematis 'Proteus'

{1876}

Pronunciation
Pro-tee-us

Heritage
Hybridizer: Charles Noble
Country of Origin: United Kingdom
Parentage: *C.* 'Fortunei' x *C. viticella* 'Rubra Grandiflora'

Growing Zones
USDA Growing Zones 4 thru 11.

Blooming Period
Early in the season and repeats.

Height Range: Five to seven feet.
Light Exposure: In hotter locales it is best planted in an area
with some shade to prevent the flowers from fading.
Pruning: Optional or light.

Highlights
Often overlooked, *C.* 'Proteus' is one of the loveliest pink
clematis. It can provide gardeners who live in colder zones
a stunning double in its first blooming cycle and single
on successive blooming cycles.

Anecdotal
In Greek mythology, Proteus was the son of Poseidon,
god of the sea. Proteus could change his shape at will,
transforming himself into wild animals
or terrible monsters instantaneously.

C. 'Proteus'

Flower Features and Plant Characteristics
The tepals are colored a delicate mauve-pink. In USDA
Zones 4 thru 9 early flowers double dramatically (with up to
100 frilly tepals) and late season flowers are single. In USDA
Zones 10 & 11 it only produces single flowers. The flower is
6" to 8" in diameter. The single flowers consist of 6 to 8
cupped tepals. Its stamens are yellow.

Clematis 'Ramona'
(syn. *C.* 'Hybrida Seiboldii')

{1888}

Pronunciation
Ra-<u>mo</u>-nah

Heritage
Hybridizer: Possibly B. Droog
Country of Origin: Holland
Parentage: Unknown

Growing Zones
USDA Growing Zones 4 thru 11.

Blooming Period
In USDA Zones 4 thru 9 later in the season and may repeat.
In USDA Zones 10 & 11 early in the season and repeats.

Height Range: Six to eight feet.
Light Exposure: It thrives equally in sunny or shady locations.
Pruning: Optional or light.

Highlights
Unbelievable beauty and great performance all in one plant, this
old but reliable clematis is moderately vigorous and very
free-flowering. It would make a fabulous addition
to any cottage garden.

Anecdotal.
Quite possibly the same clematis as 'Hybrida Seiboldii' which
was introduced by Mr. B. Droog of Boskoop, Holland in the
1870's. 'Hybrida Seiboldii' is a cross between
C. lanuginosa and *C. patens*.

C. 'Ramona'

Flower Features and Plant Characteristics
The flower's tepals are colored an attractive lavender-blue.
The flower is 6" to 8" in diameter and has 6 to 8
large overlapping, rounded tepals.
It stamens are a showy coffee color.

Clematis 'Richard Pennell'

{1974}

PRONUNCIATION
Richard Pen-nel (rhymes with fennel)

HERITAGE
Hybridizer: Walter Pennell
Country of Origin: United Kingdom
Parentage: *C.* 'Vyvyan Pennell' x *C.* 'Daniel Deronda'

GROWING ZONES
USDA Growing Zones 4 thru 11.

BLOOMING PERIOD
Early in the season and repeats.

Height Range: Six to eight feet.
Light Exposure: It thrives equally in sunny
or shady locations.
Pruning: Optional or light.

HIGHLIGHTS
This clematis is blessed with one of the prettiest crowns
of stamens. It is an exceptional clematis because of
its very free-flowering, vigorous growth. It makes
a good container selection.

ANECDOTAL
Renowned clematarian Walter Pennell named it
after his son, Richard.

C. 'Richard Pennell'

Flower Features and Plant Characteristics
The flower's tepals are rich rosy-purple. The flower is 6" to 8"
in diameter and has 6 to 8 broad and overlapping tepals
with intensely waved edges. It stamens are gold and they
form a prominent whorl.

Clematis 'Rouge Cardinal'
(syn. *C.* 'Red Cardinal')

{circa 1968}

PRONUNCIATION
Roozh Kar-din-<u>nal</u>

HERITAGE
Hybridizer: A. Girault
Country of Origin: France
Parentage: *C.* 'Poupre Mat' x *C.* 'Ville de Lyon'

GROWING ZONES
USDA Growing Zones 4 thru 11.

BLOOMING PERIOD
In USDA Zones 4 thru 9 later in the season and may repeat.
In USDA Zones 10 & 11 early in the season and repeats.

Height Range: Six to eight feet.
Light Exposure: It thrives equally in sunny
or shady locations.
Pruning: Optional or hard.

HIGHLIGHTS
The claim to fame for this outstanding clematis
is its rich, velvety color. Prolific and easy to grow,
it also makes a good container selection.

ANECDOTAL
Introduced by Jim Fisk.

C. 'Rouge Cardinal'

Flower Features and Plant Characteristics

The flower's tepals are colored a deep carmine with an attractive velvety sheen. The flower is 6" to 8" in diameter and has 6 tepals. It stamens are beige.

Clematis 'Sally Cadge'

PRONUNCIATION
Rhymes with badge

HERITAGE
Hybridizer: Frank Cadge
Country of Origin: United Kingdom
Parentage: *C.* 'Lasurstern' x *C.* 'Nelly Moser'

GROWING ZONES
USDA Growing Zones 4 thru 11.

BLOOMING PERIOD
Early in the season and repeats.

Height Range: Six to eight feet.
Light Exposure: It thrives equally in sunny
or shady locations.
Pruning: Optional or light.

HIGHLIGHTS
Although slow to start, once established it is a
moderately vigorous performer. This romantic clematis
makes a good selection for a container.

C. 'Sally Cadge'

FLOWER FEATURES AND PLANT CHARACTERISTICS
The flower's tepals are a soft lavender-blue with a carmine bar.
Bar intensity may vary from zone to zone. The flower is
5" to 7" in diameter and has 6 to 8 tepals that are
ruffled on the edges and pointed at the tips.
Its stamens are a soft beige.

Clematis 'Scartho Gem'

PRONUNCIATION
<u>Scar</u>-tho

HERITAGE
Hybridizer: Walter Pennell
Country of Origin: United Kingdom
Parentage: *C.* 'Lincoln Star' x *C.* 'Mrs. N. Thompson'

GROWING ZONES
USDA Growing Zones 4 thru 11.

BLOOMING PERIOD
Early in the season and repeats.

Height Range: Six to eight feet.
Light Exposure: In hotter locales it is best planted in an area
with some shade to prevent the flowers from fading.
Pruning: Optional or light.

HIGHLIGHTS
The attractive coloring of this clematis makes it a nice addition
to any shade garden. In USDA Zones 4 to 9 early flowers
are often semi-double and late season flowers are single.
Its compact size makes it suitable for containers.

ANECDOTAL
Scartho is the name of the Pennell's nursery where
this variety was raised in 1973.

C. 'Scartho Gem'

FLOWER FEATURES AND PLANT CHARACTERISTICS

The flower's tepals delicate pink coloring is enhanced by a stunning deeper pink central bar. The flower is 6" to 8" in diameter and has 6 to 8 wavy-edged tepals. Its stamens are reddish-brown.

Clematis 'Sealand Gem'

{1957}

PRONUNCIATION
<u>See</u>-land

HERITAGE
Hybridizer: Bees Nursery, Ltd.
Country of Origin: United Kingdom
Parentage: Unknown

GROWING ZONES
USDA Growing Zones 4 thru 11.

BLOOMING PERIOD
Early in the season and repeats.

Height Range: Six to eight feet.
Light Exposure: It thrives equally in sunny
or shady locations.
Pruning: Optional or light.

HIGHLIGHTS
One of the prettiest clematis as well as being easy to
grow, 'Sealand Gem' is a prolific bloomer. A good
suggestion would be to combine it with
Clematis viticella 'Abundance' to bring
out the rose coloring in 'Sealand Gem's
bar. Suitable for containers.

ANECDOTAL
'Sealand Gem' originated from the same crop
of seedlings from which Bees Nursery
produced 'Bees Jubilee'.

C. 'Sealand Gem'

Flower Features and Plant Characteristics

The flower's tepals are colored a sweet, pale lavender with a delicate rose bar. The flower is 4" to 6" in diameter and has 6 round overlapping tepals that are slightly rippled. It stamens are carmine.

Clematis 'Serenata'

PRONUNCIATION
Seh-reh-<u>nah</u>-tah

HERITAGE
Hybridizer: Tag Lundell
Country of Origin: Sweden
Parentage: A chance seedling of *C.* 'Madame Edouard André'

GROWING ZONES
USDA Growing Zones 4 thru 11.

BLOOMING PERIOD
Early in the season and repeats.

Height Range: Eight to ten feet.
Light Exposure: It thrives equally in sunny
or shady locations.
Pruning: Optional or light.

HIGHLIGHTS
'Serenata' is a classic climber that is vigorous and prolific.
The early blooms have 6 large tepals and later flowers
usually have 4 tepals. Grow it on a tall obelisk or arch.

ANECDOTAL
Introduced by Treasures of Tenbury which is located in
England and houses a national collection of clematis.

C. 'Serenata'

FLOWER FEATURES AND PLANT CHARACTERISTICS
The flower's tepals are colored a dusky plum-purple that
gradually darkens in the center. The flower is 4" to 6" in
diameter and has 4 to 6 tepals.
Its stamens are a contrasting yellow.

Clematis 'Sho-un'

(syn. *C.* Shoun, *C.* Sho Un)

PRONUNCIATION
Show-oon

HERITAGE
Hybridizer: General Sakurai
Country of Origin: Japan
Parentage: Unknown

GROWING ZONES
USDA Growing Zones 4 thru 11.

BLOOMING PERIOD
Early in the season and repeats.

Height Range: Six to eight feet.
Light Exposure: It thrives equally in sunny
or shady locations.
Pruning: Optional or light.

HIGHLIGHTS
The pretty stamens of this Japanese introduction add to
its graceful beauty. It would make a wonderful addition
to a small garden or container.

ANECDOTAL
The name Sho-un has been translated into English as:
"Blue Cloud" and "Cloud of Good Luck".

C. 'Sho-un'

FLOWER FEATURES AND PLANT CHARACTERISTICS
The flower's tepals are painted a lavender-blue. The flower is
7" to 9" in diameter and has 6 to 8 large overlapping tepals.
Its stamens are a creamy-yellow.

Clematis 'Silver Moon'

{1971}

HERITAGE
Hybridizer: Percy Picton
Country of Origin: United Kingdom
Parentage: Unknown

GROWING ZONES
USDA Growing Zones 4 thru 11.

BLOOMING PERIOD
Early in the season and repeats.

Height Range: Six to eight feet.
Light Exposure: In hotter locales it is best planted in an area
with some shade to prevent the flowers from fading.
Pruning: Optional or light.

HIGHLIGHTS
Bright shade emphasizes its luminescent beauty.
This very attractive clematis performs
well in a container.

ANECDOTAL
Introduced by Jim Fisk.

C. 'Silver Moon'

FLOWER FEATURES AND PLANT CHARACTERISTICS
The flower's tepals are a silver-mauve often described as Mother of Pearl. The flower is 6" to 8" in diameter and has 6 overlapping tepals. Its stamens are cream-colored.

Clematis 'Snow Queen'

{1960}

HERITAGE
Discoverer: W. S. Callick
Country of Origin: New Zealand
Parentage: Unknown

GROWING ZONES
USDA Growing Zones 4 thru 11.

BLOOMING PERIOD
Early in the season and repeats.

Height Range: Six to eight feet.
Light Exposure: It thrives equally in sunny
or shady locations.
Pruning: Optional or light.

HIGHLIGHTS
'Snow Queen' has exquisitely formed flowers and
is a good free-flowering cultivar. It would bring
elegance to any bridal bouquet.

ANECDOTAL
Introduced by Alister Keay.

C. 'Snow Queen'

FLOWER FEATURES AND PLANT CHARACTERISTICS
The flower's tepals are snow-white with mauve-pink bars
that fade with age. The flowers are 6" to 8" in diameter
and face skyward. It produces 6 to 8 tepals with
pointed tips and rippled edges.
Its stamens are a deep reddish-brown.

Clematis 'Star of India'

{1867}

HERITAGE
Hybridizer: Thomas Cripps & Son.
Country of Origin: United Kingdom
Parentage: *C. lanuginosa* x *C.* 'Jackmanii'

GROWING ZONES
USDA Growing Zones 4 thru 11.

BLOOMING PERIOD
In USDA Zones 4 thru 9 later in the season and may repeat.
In USDA Zones 10 & 11 early in the season and repeats.

Height Range: Ten to twelve (possibly taller) feet.
Light Exposure: It thrives equally in sunny
or shady locations.
Pruning: Optional or hard.

HIGHLIGHTS
'Star of India's flowers are blessed with a voluptuous hue.
Pair it with a climbing pink rose like 'Gertrude Jekyll'
for a stunning combination. This is a tall clematis which
can grow over an arch. It will also take the
heat of warmer locales.

C. 'Star of India'

FLOWER FEATURES AND PLANT CHARACTERISTICS
The flower's tepals are a stunning reddish-plum decorated
with a carmine bar. The flower is 4" to 6" in diameter
and has 4 to 6 overlapping tepals.
Its stamens are pale yellow.

Clematis 'Sugar Candy'
(syn. *C.* 'Evione')

{circa 1990}

HERITAGE
Hybridizer: Raymond Evison
Country of Origin: United Kingdom
Parentage: Unknown

GROWING ZONES
USDA Growing Zones 4 thru 11.

BLOOMING PERIOD
Early in the season and repeats.

Height Range: Six to eight feet.
Light Exposure: It thrives equally in sunny
or shady locations.
Pruning: Optional or light.

HIGHLIGHTS
Very large flowers grace this scrumptious clematis.
It is a fabulous choice for a cut flower because
of its long-lasting ability.

C. 'Sugar Candy'

FLOWER FEATURES AND PLANT CHARACTERISTICS
The flower's tepals are a cheery pinkish-mauve with a darker
central bar. The flower is 7" to 8" in diameter and has
6 to 7 pointed tepals. Its stamens are yellow.

Clematis 'Sunset'

{circa 1990}

HERITAGE
Hybridizer: Arthur H. Steffen
Country of Origin: U.S.A
Parentage: Unknown

GROWING ZONES
USDA Growing Zones 4 thru 11.

BLOOMING PERIOD
Early in the season and repeats.

Height Range: Six to eight feet.
Light Exposure: It thrives equally in sunny
or shady locations.
Pruning: Optional or light.

HIGHLIGHTS
Alluring coloring combined with moderate growth
makes it an excellent choice for a container.
Repeats nicely.

ANECDOTAL
This American clematis is Arthur Steffen's second
large-flowered hybrid clematis introduction. He
raised it in the late 1980's.

C. 'Sunset'
FLOWER FEATURES AND PLANT CHARACTERISTICS
The flower's tepals are tinted a stunning magenta. The flower is
4" to 6" in diameter and has 6 to 8 tepals.
It stamens are bright yellow.

Clematis texensis 'Duchess of Albany'
(syn. *C.* 'Duchess of Albany')

{1894}

Pronunciation
teck-<u>sen</u>-siss

Heritage
Hybridizer: Arthur George Jackman
Country of Origin: United Kingdom
Parentage: *C.* 'Star of India' x *C. texensis*

Growing Zones
USDA Growing Zones 4 thru 11.

Blooming Period
In USDA Zones 4 thru 9 later in the season and may repeat.
In USDA Zones 10 & 11 mid season and repeats.

Height Range: Eight to ten feet.
Light Exposure: It prefers a sunny location.
Pruning: Hard. It will die to the ground in the colder zones.

Highlights
'Duchess of Albany' will decorate your garden with hundreds of
sweet pink "tulip twins" that face skywards. Charming, vigorous
and easy to grow, be sure it has a tall trellis to call home.

Anecdotal
Arthur George Jackman crossed the 'Star of India' with the
American native species *texensis* creating 6 new cultivars known as
the Wokingensis Hybrids. *C. texensis* 'Duchess of Albany' and
texensis 'Sir Trevor Lawrence' may be the only two
Wokingensis Hybrids still in existence.

C. texensis 'Duchess of Albany'

Flower Features and Plant Characteristics
The flower's tepals are colored a vivid pink with a central
cherry-red bar that form tulip-like flowers. The flower is 2"
to 3" in diameter and has 4 tepals. Its stamens are yellow.

Clematis texensis 'Gravetye Beauty'

(syn. *C.* 'Gravetye Beauty')

{1914}

Pronunciation
teck-<u>sen</u>-siss <u>Grave</u>-tie

Heritage
Hybridizer: Frances (Francisque) Morel
Country of Origin: France
Parentage: Possibly a cross with a *C. texensis*

Growing Zones
USDA Growing Zones 4 thru 11.

Blooming Period
In USDA Zones 4 thru 9 later in the season and may repeat.
In USDA Zones 10 & 11 mid season and repeats.

Height Range: Six to ten feet.
Light Exposure: It prefers a sunny location.
Pruning: Hard. It will die to the ground in the colder zones.

Highlights
This clematis really is a scarlet beauty. Enjoy the show as the blooms take their journey from bud to a full fledged star-shaped star of a clematis. 'Gravetye Beauty' is the clematis that comes closest to reflecting a true red.

Anecdotal
Named after Gravetye Manor, the large estate of William Robinson in Sussex, England. Head Gardener Ernest Markham along with Mr. Robinson raised it from seedlings produced by Frances Morel.

C. texensis 'Gravetye Beauty'

Flower Features and Plant Characteristics
The flower's tepals are colored a bright crimson-red. The flower is
2½" to 3" in diameter and has 4 to 6 trumpet shaped tepals that
gradually open into a star-like flower. It stamens are yellow.

Clematis texensis
'Sir Trevor Lawrence'
(syn. *C.* 'Sir Trevor Lawrence')

{1895}

PRONUNCIATION
teck-<u>sen</u>-siss

HERITAGE
Hybridizer: Arthur George Jackman
Country of Origin: United Kingdom
Parentage: *C.* 'Star of India' x *C. texensis*

GROWING ZONES
USDA Growing Zones 4 thru 11.

BLOOMING PERIOD
In USDA Zones 4 thru 9 later in the season and may repeat.
In USDA Zones 10 & 11 mid season and repeats.

Height Range: Six to eight feet.
Light Exposure: It prefers a sunny location.
Pruning: Hard. It will die to the ground in the colder zones.

HIGHLIGHTS
Its mesmerizing coloring makes it an alluring choice for any garden.
A clematis for connoisseurs, it is ideal for container gardening.

ANECDOTAL
Named in honor of the past president of the Royal Horticultural
Society who was a distinguished grower and breeder of orchids.
'Sir Trevor Lawrence' along with 'Duchess of Albany' are thought
to be the only remaining Wokingensis Hybrids.

C. texensis 'Sir Trevor Lawrence'

FLOWER FEATURES AND PLANT CHARACTERISTICS

The flower's tepals are brushed a bright reddish-violet with a red central bar forming tulip-like flowers that face skywards. The flower is 2" in diameter and has 4 tepals. Its stamens are yellow.

Clematis 'The President'
(syn. *C.* 'President')

{circa 1876}

HERITAGE
Hybridizer: Charles Noble
Country of Origin: United Kingdom
Parentage: *C.* 'Jackmanii' x *C. patens*.

GROWING ZONES
USDA Growing Zones 4 thru 11.

BLOOMING PERIOD
Early in the season and repeats.

Height Range: Six to ten feet.
Light Exposure: It thrives equally in sunny
or shady locations.
Pruning: Optional or light.

HIGHLIGHTS
This elder statesman's long-lived popularity can be
attributed to its extensive flowering ability. It is also
dependable and easy to grow. Since the flowers face
skyward, it is a nice choice to
train on a low fence.

C. 'The President'

Flower Features and Plant Characteristics

The flower's tepals are colored a vibrant purple-blue. The flower is 6" to 8" in diameter and has 8 overlapping tepals that form a partially cupped bloom. Its stamens are reddish-purple.

Clematis triternata x
'Rubromarginata'

(syn. *C. triternata* 'Rubro marginata', *C.* 'Triternata Rubromarginata')

PRONUNCIATION
try-tur-<u>nay</u>-ta Roo-bro-mar-gin-<u>nay</u>-ta

HERITAGE
Hybridizer: Thomas Cripps
Country of Origin: United Kingdom
Parentage: *C. flammula* x *C. viticella*

GROWING ZONES
USDA Growing Zones 4 thru 11.

BLOOMING PERIOD
Late in the season and may repeat

Height Range: Eight to twelve feet.
Light Exposure: It thrives equally in sunny
or shady locations.
Pruning: Optional or hard.

HIGHLIGHTS
This clematis produces clouds of starry blossoms. In the colder
locales of Zones 4 thru 9 it will yield a fragrance that is
described as "marzipan." A nice candidate for an arch.

ANECDOTAL
Its long name is based on the following botanical terms:
"Tri", when in compound words signifying three; "Ternata",
meaning with parts in groups of three, referring often to the
leaflets; "Rubro", meaning red; "Marginata", meaning
margined by another color.

226

C. triternata x 'Rubromarginata'

FLOWER FEATURES AND PLANT CHARACTERISTICS
The flower's tepals are colored white and edged with
mauve-pink. The flower is 1" to 2" in diameter and has
4 to 6 tiny star-shaped tepals. Its stamens are yellow.

Clematis 'Victoria'

{1870}

HERITAGE
Hybridizer: Thomas Cripps
Country of Origin: United Kingdom
Parentage: *C.* 'Jackmanii' x *C. lanuginosa*

GROWING ZONES
USDA Growing Zones 4 thru 11.

BLOOMING PERIOD
In USDA Zones 4 thru 9 later in the season and may repeat.
In USDA Zones 10 & 11 early in the season and repeats.

Height Range: Eight to ten (possibly twelve) feet.
Light Exposure: It thrives equally in sunny
or shady locations.
Pruning: Optional or hard.

HIGHLIGHTS
A real workhorse, 'Victoria' is one of the most dependable
and easily grown clematis. I highly recommended it
for gardens that are in hot locales. It is an excellent
choice to cover an arch.

C. 'Victoria'

FLOWER FEATURES AND PLANT CHARACTERISTICS
The flower's tepals are brushed with a soft rosy-purple color and include 3 midribs all blanketed by a unique textured surface. The flower is 4" to 6" in diameter and has 4 to 6 tepals. Its stamens are buff-colored.

Clematis 'Ville de Lyon'

{1899}

PRONUNCIATION
Veel duh Lee-<u>own</u>

HERITAGE
Hybridizer: Frances (Francisque) Morel
Country of Origin: France
Parentage: *C.* 'Viviand Morel' x *C. texensis*

GROWING ZONES
USDA Growing Zones 4 thru 11.

BLOOMING PERIOD
In USDA Zones 4 thru 9 later in the season and may repeat.
In USDA Zones 10 & 11 early in the season and repeats.

Height Range: Seven to ten feet.
Light Exposure: It performs best when planted
in an area with some direct sun.
Pruning: Optional or hard.

HIGHLIGHTS
This clematis can best be described as having something
for everyone. It is both beautiful and unique. Each tepal
is highlighted with an opalescent sheen. This clematis
can stand alone or be combined nicely with a
contrasting colored clematis.

ANECDOTAL
Mr. Morel named this clematis after his hometown.
Ville de Lyon means city of the lion.

C. 'Ville de Lyon'

FLOWER FEATURES AND PLANT CHARACTERISTICS

The flower's tepals are colored a deep candy-apple red on the outer edges with a crimson bar in the center. The flower is 4" to 6" in diameter and has 6 tepals.
Its stamens are a creamy yellow.

Clematis 'Violet Elizabeth'

{1974}

HERITAGE
Hybridizer: Walter Pennell
Country of Origin: United Kingdom
Parentage: *C.* 'Vyvyan Pennell' x *C.* 'Mrs. Spencer Castle'.

GROWING ZONES
USDA Growing Zones 4 thru 11.

BLOOMING PERIOD
Early in the season and repeats.

Height Range: Six to eight feet.
Light Exposure: In hotter locales it is best to plant it in an
area with some shade to prevent the flowers from fading.
Pruning: Optional or light.

HIGHLIGHTS
This double flower is reminiscent of a ballerina's frilly
skirt. Although this pretty pink clematis can be slow to
become established, your patience will be rewarded.
Perfect for containers.

ANECDOTAL
Mr. Pennell named this clematis after Violet Smith,
a loyal employee who worked at the Pennell office.

C. 'Violet Elizabeth'

FLOWER FEATURES AND PLANT CHARACTERISTICS
The flower's tepals are colored an attractive mauve-pink.
The flower is 4" to 6" in diameter. Its stamens are yellow.

Clematis viticella 'Abundance'

(syn. *C.* 'Abundance')

{1939}

HERITAGE
Hybridizer: Frances (Francisque) Morel
Country of Origin: France
Parentage: Unknown

GROWING ZONES
USDA Growing Zones 4 thru 11.

BLOOMING PERIOD
In USDA Zones 4 thru 9 later in the season and may repeat.
In USDA Zones 10 & 11 later in the season and repeats.

Height Range: Six to nine feet.
Light Exposure: It thrives equally in sunny
or shady locations.
Pruning: Optional or hard.

HIGHLIGHTS
Aptly named, this clematis produces an amazing
"abundance" of textured flowers. Perfect when combined
with a large flowering hybrid because the contrasting
sizes make quite an eye-appealing statement.

ANECDOTAL
It was named and introduced by George Jackman
& Son Nursery.

C. viticella 'Abundance'

FLOWER FEATURES AND PLANT CHARACTERISTICS
The flower's tepals are painted a bright mauve-pink. The flower is
2" is to 2½" in diameter and has 4 to 6 distinctly textured tepals.
Its stamens are greenish-yellow.

Clematis viticella 'Alba Luxurians'

(syn. *C.* 'Alba Luxurians')

{circa 1900}

PRONUNCIATION
Al-ba Lug-zhur-ree-ons

HERITAGE
Hybridizer: Robert Veitch & Son
Country of Origin: United Kingdom
Parentage: Unknown

Growing Zones
USDA Growing Zones 4 thru 11.

BLOOMING PERIOD
In USDA Zones 4 thru 9 later in the season and may repeat.
In USDA Zones 10 & 11 later in the season and repeats.

Height Range: Seven to ten feet.
Light Exposure: It thrives equally in sunny
or shady locations.
Pruning: Optional or hard.

HIGHLIGHTS
It produces myriads of luxurious nodding flowers. It is
very dependable and a prolific bloomer. Its beauty shines
when combined with another companion plant.

ANECDOTAL
Its name is based on two botanical terms:
"alba", meaning white and
"luxurians", meaning luxuriant.

C. viticella 'Alba Luxurians'

FLOWER FEATURES AND PLANT CHARACTERISTICS
The flower's tepals are colored creamy white. Early flower's tepals are often tipped with green. The flower is 2½" to 3" in diameter and has 4 to 5 tepals. Its stamens are a dark purple creating a nice contrast.

Clematis viticella 'Betty Corning'
(syn. *C.* 'Betty Corning')

{circa 1933}

HERITAGE
Hybridizer: Unknown
Discovered by: Elizabeth (Betty) Corning
Introduced by: Arthur H. Steffen
Country of Origin: U.S.A.
Parentage: *C. crispa* x *C. viticella* (possibly)

GROWING ZONES
USDA Growing Zones 4 thru 11.

BLOOMING PERIOD
In USDA Zones 4 thru 9 later in the season and may repeat.
In USDA Zones 10 & 11 later in the season and repeats.

Height Range: Six to nine feet.
Light Exposure: It thrives equally in sunny or shady locations.
Pruning: Optional or hard.

HIGHLIGHTS
Its charming nodding bells make it a welcome addition
to any garden. In the colder locales of
USDA Zones 4 to 9 it has a fragrance.

ANECDOTAL
The first American cultivar, it is named after the well-respected
horticulturist, Mrs. Betty Corning. The exact specifics of its
heritage are unclear but it is believed to be a cross between
C. crispa x *C. viticella*. It is fitting that it is our first cultivar
since one of the presumed birth parents, *Clematis crispa*,
is our first American species.

C. viticella 'Betty Corning'

FLOWER FEATURES AND PLANT CHARACTERISTICS
The flower's tepals are colored a soft lavender-mauve and form a small nodding bell. The flower is 1½" (occasionally up to 2") in diameter. Its stamens are yellow.

Clematis viticella 'Blue Angel'

(syn. *C.* 'Blekitny Aniol', *C.* 'Blue Angel')

{1988}

HERITAGE
Hybridizer: Brother Stefan Franczak
Country of Origin: Poland
Parentage: Unknown

GROWING ZONES
USDA Growing Zones 4 thru 11.

BLOOMING PERIOD
In USDA Zones 4 thru 9 later in the season and may repeat.
In USDA Zones 10 & 11 later in the season and repeats.

Height Range: Six to nine feet.
Light Exposure: It thrives equally in sunny
or shady locations.
Pruning: Optional or hard.

HIGHLIGHTS
Grow this *viticella* for its pastel coloring and
uniquely-shaped flowers. It makes a good choice
for a tall obelisk.

ANECDOTAL
'Blekitny Aniol' is Polish for "blue angel."

C. viticella 'Blue Angel'

FLOWER FEATURES AND PLANT CHARACTERISTICS

The flower's tepals are colored a clear lavender-blue. The flower is 3" to 4" in diameter and has 4 to 6 tepals with delicate wavy edges. Its stamens are yellow.

Clematis viticella 'Blue Belle'

(syn. *C.* 'Blue Belle')

{circa 1937}

HERITAGE
Hybridizer: George Jackman & Son
Country of Origin: United Kingdom
Parentage: Unknown

GROWING ZONES
USDA Growing Zones 4 thru 11.

BLOOMING PERIOD
In USDA Zones 4 thru 9 later in the season and may repeat.
In USDA Zones 10 & 11 later in the season and repeats.

Height Range: Seven to ten feet.
Light Exposure: It thrives equally in sunny
or shady locations.
Pruning: Optional or hard.

HIGHLIGHTS
Even though its flowers are not a true blue as its name
implies, you can not go wrong with this vigorous *viticella*.
A very dependable bloomer.

ANECDOTAL
The word "belle" means beautiful.

C. viticella 'Blue Belle'

FLOWER FEATURES AND PLANT CHARACTERISTICS
The flower's tepals are tinted a deep purple-blue. The flower is
3" to 4" in diameter and has 4 to 6 tepals.
Its stamens are yellow.

Clematis viticella 'Carmencita'

(syn. *C.* 'Carmencita')

PRONUNCIATION
Car-men-<u>see</u>-tah

HERITAGE
Hybridizer: Magnus Johnson
Country of Origin: Sweden
Parentage: From a seedling of *C. viticella* 'Grandiflora Sanguinea'

GROWING ZONES
USDA Growing Zones 4 thru 11.

BLOOMING PERIOD
In USDA Zones 4 thru 9 later in the season and may repeat.
In USDA Zones 10 & 11 later in the season and repeats.

Height Range: Six to eight feet.
Light Exposure: It thrives equally in sunny
or shady locations.
Pruning: Optional or hard.

HIGHLIGHTS
Attractive coloring and diminutive size makes this an
outstanding clematis.

ANECDOTAL
Mr. Johnson raised this clematis in 1952 choosing the
name 'Carmencita' because it reminded him of
"dark-eyed Spanish beauties."

C. viticella 'Carmencita'

FLOWER FEATURES AND PLANT CHARACTERISTICS
The flower's tepals are colored a vivid reddish-purple. The flower
is 2" to 2½" in diameter and has 4 to 6 satiny tepals that are
semi-nodding. Its stamens are dark purple.

Clematis viticella 'Emilia Plater'

(syn. *C.* 'Emilia Plater')

{1986}

PRONUNCIATION
Em-meel-lee-ah Plat-ter

HERITAGE
Hybridizer: Brother Stefan Franczak
Country of Origin: Poland
Parentage: Unknown

GROWING ZONES
USDA Growing Zones 4 thru 11.

BLOOMING PERIOD
In USDA Zones 4 thru 9 later in the season and may repeat.
In USDA Zones 10 & 11 later in the season and repeats.

Height Range: Six to nine feet.
Light Exposure: It thrives equally in sunny
or shady locations.
Pruning: Optional or hard.

HIGHLIGHTS
Grow this clematis for its delicate beauty
and elegantly formed flowers.

ANECDOTAL
This clematis honors the Polish heroine, Emilia Plater
(1806-1831), who died at the age of 25 during the
Polish uprising against Russian occupation.

C. viticella 'Emilia Plater'

FLOWER FEATURES AND PLANT CHARACTERISTICS

The flower's tepals are colored a soft violet-blue. The flower is 3" to 4" in diameter and has 4 to 5 wavy tepals with a texture similar to crêpe paper. Its stamens are creamy-yellow.

Clematis viticella 'Etoile Violette'

(syn. *C.* 'Violet Star')

{1885}

PRONUNCIATION
Ay-twal Vee-o-<u>let</u>

HERITAGE
Hybridizer: Frances (Francisque) Morel
Country of Origin: France
Parentage: Unknown

GROWING ZONES
USDA Growing Zones 4 thru 11.

BLOOMING PERIOD
In USDA Zones 4 thru 9 later in the season and may repeat.
In USDA Zones 10 & 11 later in the season and repeats.

Height Range: Six to nine feet.
Light Exposure: It thrives equally in sunny
or shady locations.
Pruning: Optional or hard.

HIGHLIGHTS
This extraordinary clematis is revered for its profusion of
blooms over an extended period of time. Dependable
because of its trouble-free and vigorous nature. A
perfect choice for warmer locales.

ANECDOTAL
'Etoile Violette' is French for "violet star."

C. viticella 'Etoile Violette'

FLOWER FEATURES AND PLANT CHARACTERISTICS
The flower's tepals are a beautiful rich reddish-purple. The nodding flower is 2½" to 3½" in diameter and has 4 to 6 textured tepals. Its stamens are yellow.

Clematis viticella 'Flore Pleno'

(syn. *C.* 'Flore Pleno' or *C.* 'Mary Rose')

PRONUNCIATION
Floor-eh Play-no

HERITAGE
Hybridizer: Unknown
Country of Origin: United Kingdom
Parentage: Unknown

GROWING ZONES
USDA Growing Zones 4 thru 11.

BLOOMING PERIOD
In USDA Zones 4 thru 9 later in the season and may repeat.
In USDA Zones 10 & 11 later in the season and repeats.

Height Range: Six to nine feet.
Light Exposure: It thrives equally in sunny
or shady locations.
Pruning: Optional or hard.

HIGHLIGHTS
Its coloring can best be compared to that of an amethyst
gemstone. The flowers always double.

C. viticella 'Flore Pleno'
FLOWER FEATURES AND PLANT CHARACTERISTICS
The flower's tepals are a pale amethyst. The flower is
2" in diameter and has tepals that form a double flower that
resembles small pompom mums. Its stamens are not visible.

Clematis viticella 'Kermesina'
(syn. *C.* 'Kermesina' or *C. viticella* 'Rubra')

{1883}

PRONUNCIATION
Ker-mess-<u>see</u>-nah

HERITAGE
Hybridizer: Victor Lemoine & Son
Country of Origin: France
Parentage: Unknown

GROWING ZONES
USDA Growing Zones 4 thru 11.

BLOOMING PERIOD
In USDA Zones 4 thru 9 later in the season and may repeat.
In USDA Zones 10 & 11 later in the season and repeats.

Height Range: Six to nine feet.
Light Exposure: It thrives equally in sunny
or shady locations.
Pruning: Optional or hard.

HIGHLIGHTS
This little gem of a *viticella* shines like a ruby in your
garden. Grow it on a tall trellis.

ANECDOTAL
This clematis received its named because it reminded
Mr. Lemoine of the red dye-producing scale insect kermes.

C. viticella 'Kermesina'

FLOWER FEATURES AND PLANT CHARACTERISTICS
The flower's tepals are colored a clear reddish-mauve with a
small white dot at each base. The flower is 2½" to 3" in diameter
and has 4 to 5 tepals. Its stamens are reddish-purple.

Clematis viticella 'Little Nell'

(syn. *C.* 'Little Nell')

{circa 1939}

HERITAGE
Hybridizer: Frances (Francisque) Morel
Country of Origin: France
Parentage: Unknown

GROWING ZONES
USDA Growing Zones 4 thru 11.

BLOOMING PERIOD
In USDA Zones 4 thru 9 later in the season and may repeat.
In USDA Zones 10 & 11 later in the season and repeats.

Height Range: Six to nine feet.
Light Exposure: It thrives equally in sunny
or shady locations.
Pruning: Optional or hard.

HIGHLIGHTS
This delicate flower needs to be planted in a location
that is easily viewed or its subtle beauty may be lost.
Would make a romantic addition to
a bridal bouquet.

ANECDOTAL
Ernest Markham named this clematis after
his wife, Nell.

C. viticella 'Little Nell'

FLOWER FEATURES AND PLANT CHARACTERISTICS

The flower's tepals are painted a soft creamy-white and are outlined with a very soft violet margin. The flower is 2" to 2½" in diameter and has 4 to 6 tepals. Its stamens are light green.

Clematis viticella
'Madame Julia Correvon'
(syn. *C.* 'Madame Julia Correvon')

{circa 1900}

PRONUNCIATION
Mah-<u>dahm</u> or Ma-<u>dom</u> Julia Cor-rev-<u>vone</u> (rhymes with phone)

HERITAGE
Hybridizer: Frances (Francisque) Morel
Country of Origin: France
Parentage: *C.* 'Ville de Lyon' x *C. viticella* 'Rubra Grandiflora'

GROWING ZONES
USDA Growing Zones 4 thru 11.

BLOOMING PERIOD
In USDA Zones 4 thru 9 later in the season and may repeat.
In USDA Zones 10 & 11 later in the season and repeats.

Height Range: Six to nine feet.
Light Exposure: It thrives equally in sunny or shady locations.
Pruning: Optional or hard.

HIGHLIGHTS
Always getting rave reviews, this is a compact *viticella*
that is a perennial favorite of clematis gardeners.
Does well in containers.

ANECDOTAL
Mr. Morel named it in honor of a member of the
Correvon family of nurserymen.

C. viticella 'Madame Julia Correvon'

FLOWER FEATURES AND PLANT CHARACTERISTICS
The flower's tepals are tinted a clear wine-red. The flower is
3" to 4" in diameter and usually has 4 to 6 tepals that can
be uniquely twisted. Its stamens are golden.

Clematis viticella 'Margot Koster'

(syn. *C.* 'Margot Koster', *C.* 'M. Koster')

{circa 1895}

PRONUNCIATION
Mar-go Koss-ter

HERITAGE
Hybridizer: Marinus Koster
Country of Origin: Holland
Parentage: *C. patens* x unknown *C. viticella*

GROWING ZONES
USDA Growing Zones 4 thru 11.

BLOOMING PERIOD
In USDA Zones 4 thru 9 later in the season and may repeat.
In USDA Zones 10 & 11 later in the season and repeats.

Height Range: Six to nine feet.
Light Exposure: It thrives equally in sunny
or shady locations.
Pruning: Optional or hard.

HIGHLIGHTS
One of the prettiest of the pink clematis, its good looks
are accentuated by its uniquely shaped blooms.

ANECDOTAL
Named after a family member of the raiser,
Marinus Koster.

C. viticella 'Margot Koster'

FLOWER FEATURES AND PLANT CHARACTERISTICS
The flower's tepals are sprayed a striking bright pink. The flower is 3" to 4" in diameter and has 4 to 6 twisted tepals that roll back. Its stamens are yellow.

259

Clematis viticella 'Minuet'

(syn. *C.* 'Minuet')

{1952}

PRONUNCIATION
Min-you-<u>et</u>

HERITAGE
Hybridizer: Frances (Francisque) Morel
Country of Origin: France
Parentage: Unknown

GROWING ZONES
USDA Growing Zones 4 thru 11.

BLOOMING PERIOD
In USDA Zones 4 thru 9 later in the season and may repeat.
In USDA Zones 10 & 11 later in the season and repeats.

Height Range: Six to nine feet.
Light Exposure: It thrives equally in sunny
or shady locations.
Pruning: Optional or hard.

HIGHLIGHTS
This graceful French beauty is a reliable performer. Its
dainty flowers dance in the breeze.

ANECDOTAL
Raised circa 1900 and named by Ernest Markham. It was
introduced by George Jackman. The minuet is a graceful
dance and is an appropriate namesake for
this diminutive beauty.

C. viticella 'Minuet'

FLOWER FEATURES AND PLANT CHARACTERISTICS

The flower's tepals are painted a soft cream and are bordered
with a deep mauve margin. The flower is 1½" to 2½" in
diameter and has 4 tepals with mauve veins.
Its stamens are green.

Clematis viticella 'Pagoda'

(syn. *C. texensis* 'Pagoda', *C.* 'Pagoda')

{1983}

Pronunciation
Pa-go-da

Heritage
Hybridizer: Raised by John Treasure
Country of Origin: United Kingdom
Parentage: *C. texensis* 'Etoile Rose' x *C. viticella*

Growing Zones
USDA Growing Zones 4 thru 11.

Blooming Period
In USDA Zones 4 thru 9 later in the season and may repeat.
In USDA Zones 10 & 11 later in the season and repeats.

Height Range: Six to eight feet.
Light Exposure: It thrives equally in sunny or shady locations.
Pruning: Optional or hard.

Highlights
This cute little treasure sways in the breeze making it a
tranquil addition to the garden. Its profile resembles
a garden pavilion roof.

Anecdotal
Most often sold in this country as *C. texensis* 'Pagoda', there is
some debate whether it is a texensis or a viticella type. Many
still refer to the breeder's original classification but, since
there is more viticella blood in its heritage, I am
including it in the viticella group.

C. viticella 'Pagoda'
Flower Features and Plant Characteristics
The upper sides of the flower's tepals are painted white with
mauve-pink edges and veining. The undersides are mauve-pink
with a dark purple center bar. The flower is 1½" to 3" in
diameter and has 4 tepals that twist with age.
Its stamens are creamy-yellow.

Clematis viticella
'Purpurea Plena Elegans'

(syn. *C.* 'Plena Elegans')

PRONUNCIATION
Purr-<u>purr</u>-ee-a Play-na El-leg-ganz

HERITAGE
Hybridizer: Frances (Francisque) Morel
Country of Origin: France
Parentage: Unknown

GROWING ZONES
USDA Growing Zones 4 thru 11.

BLOOMING PERIOD
In USDA Zones 4 thru 9 later in the season and may repeat.
In USDA Zones 10 & 11 later in the season and repeats.

Height Range: Six to nine feet.
Light Exposure: It thrives equally in sunny
or shady locations.
Pruning: Optional or hard.

HIGHLIGHTS
This viticella produces masses of spectacular
chrysanthemum-like blooms.

ANECDOTAL
Horticulturally speaking, *flore plena* means
with double flowers.

C. viticella 'Purpurea Plena Elegans'

The flower's tepals form a fascinating double rosette and are colored a soft rosy-purple. The flower is 2" to 2½" in diameter. Its stamens are not visible.

Clematis viticella 'Royal Velours'

(syn. *C.* 'Royal Velours')

{1939}

PRONUNCIATION
Royal Veh-<u>loor</u>

HERITAGE
Hybridizer: Frances (Francisque) Morel
Country of Origin: France
Parentage: Unknown

GROWING ZONES
USDA Growing Zones 4 thru 11.

BLOOMING PERIOD
In USDA Zones 4 thru 9 later in the season and may repeat.
In USDA Zones 10 & 11 later in the season and repeats.

Height Range: Seven to nine feet.
Light Exposure: It thrives equally in sunny
or shady locations.
Pruning: Optional or hard.

HIGHLIGHTS
This noble viticella's tepals have a smooth soft surface that
is reminiscent of velvet. It is also blessed with lovely
flowers and delicate foliage.

ANECDOTAL
"Velours" is French for velvet, which aptly describes
the texture of the flower's surface.

C. viticella 'Royal Velours'

FLOWER FEATURES AND PLANT CHARACTERISTICS
The flower's tepals are tinted a velvety reddish-purple.
The semi-nodding flower is 2" to 3" in diameter and has
4 to 6 tepals. Its stamens are green.

Clematis viticella 'Södertälje'
(syn. *C.* 'Södertälje')

PRONUNCIATION
Suh-dirt-tell-ya

HERITAGE
Hybridizer: Magnus Johnson
Country of Origin: Sweden
Parentage: A seedling of *C. viticella* 'Grandiflora Sanguinea'

GROWING ZONES
USDA Growing Zones 4 thru 11.

BLOOMING PERIOD
In USDA Zones 4 thru 9 later in the season and may repeat.
In USDA Zones 10 & 11 later in the season and repeats.

Height Range: Six to nine feet.
Light Exposure: It thrives equally in sunny
or shady locations.
Pruning: Optional or hard.

HIGHLIGHTS
A true treasure because of it unique and beguiling flowers.
Stunning when combined with a light pink rose.

ANECDOTAL
'Södertälje' is named after the town where
Mr. Johnson's nursery is located.

C. viticellla 'Södertälje'

FLOWER FEATURES AND PLANT CHARACTERISTICS
The flower's tepals are colored a pretty pinkish-red and
the tips are often tinged with green. The semi-nodding
flower is 3" to 4" in diameter and has 4 to 6 twisted tepals.
Its stamens are greenish-yellow.

Clematis viticella 'Venosa Violacea'

(syn. *C.* 'Venosa Violacea', *C.* 'Violet Star Gazer')

{1883}

PRONUNCIATION
Ven-<u>no</u>-sa Vee-o-<u>lay</u>-se- a

HERITAGE
Hybridizer: Victor Lemoine & Sons
Country of Origin: France
Parentage: Unknown

GROWING ZONES
USDA Growing Zones 4 thru 11.

BLOOMING PERIOD
In USDA Zones 4 thru 9 later in the season and may repeat.
In USDA Zones 10 & 11 later in the season and repeats.

Height Range: Six to nine feet.
Light Exposure: It thrives equally in sunny
or shady locations.
Pruning: Optional or hard.

HIGHLIGHTS
Greatly admired for its stunning two-toned colored flowers,
it is one of the most attractive and largest of the viticellas.
Vigorous and free-flowering.

ANECDOTAL
Venosa means "veined" and
violacea denotes "violet colored."

C. viticella 'Venosa Violacea'

FLOWER FEATURES AND PLANT CHARACTERISTICS
The flower's tepals are a soft, creamy white with purple veins that are outlined with a deep violet margin. The flower is 4" in diameter and has 4 to 6 tepals. Its stamens are dark purple.

Clematis 'Voluceau'

{circa 1970}

PRONUNCIATION
Vo-loo-<u>sew</u>

HERITAGE
Hybridizer: A. Girault
Country of Origin: France
Parentage: *C.* 'Poupre Mat' x *C.* 'Ville de Lyon'.

GROWING ZONES
USDA Growing Zones 4 thru 11.

BLOOMING PERIOD
In USDA Zones 4 thru 9 later in the season and may repeat.
In USDA Zones 10 & 11 later in the season and repeats.

Height Range: Six to ten feet.
Light Exposure: It thrives equally in sunny
or shady locations.
Pruning: Optional or hard.

HIGHLIGHTS
Its captivating color combination makes it a striking
addition to any garden. This free bloomer makes an
excellent choice to mingle with
low-growing shrubs.

C. 'Voluceau'

Flower Features and Plant Characteristics
The flower's tepals are tinted dark red with a reddish-purple
central bar. The flower is 6" to 7" in diameter and has 6 tepals.
Its stamens are yellow.

Clematis 'W. E. Gladstone'

(syn. *C.* 'William Gladstone')

{1881}

PRONUNCIATION
Glad-stone

HERITAGE
Hybridizer: Charles Noble
Country of Origin: United Kingdom
Parentage: Unknown

GROWING ZONES
USDA Growing Zones 4 thru 11.

BLOOMING PERIOD
Early in the season and repeats.

Height Range: Six to eight feet.
Light Exposure: It thrives equally in sunny
or shady locations.
Pruning: Optional or light.

HIGHLIGHTS
This tried-and-true clematis is free-flowering, vigorous
and produces attractive large blossoms.

ANECDOTAL
Charles Noble named this clematis after the then
British Prime Minister, William Ewart Gladstone.

C. 'W. E. Gladstone'

FLOWER FEATURES AND PLANT CHARACTERISTICS
The flower's tepals are brushed with a lilac-blue coloring. The flower is 6" to 8" in diameter and has 6 to 8 very large tepals. Its stamens are reddish-brown.

Clematis 'Wada's Primrose'

(syn. *C. patens* 'Mandshu-Kii')

{1965}

PRONUNCIATION
Wah-duh

HERITAGE
Country of Origin: Manchuria
Parentage: Unknown

GROWING ZONES
USDA Growing Zones 4 thru 11.

BLOOMING PERIOD
Early in the season and repeats.

Height Range: Six to eight feet.
Light Exposure: It is best planted in an area with some
shade to prevent the flowers from fading.
Pruning: Optional or light.

HIGHLIGHTS
The delicate cream coloring of this clematis can brighten a
shady area in the garden. Perfect for a container.

ANECDOTAL
Kii is Japanese for yellow . Said to have a slight citrus
fragrance on warm days. Sold in The U.S. primarily
under the name 'Wada's Primrose'.

C. 'Wada's Primrose'

FLOWER FEATURES AND PLANT CHARACTERISTICS
The flower's tepals are a soft creamy-yellow that matures to
cream. The flower is 6" to 7" in diameter and has 8 tepals.
Its stamens are yellow.

Clematis 'Walter Pennell'

PRONUNCIATION
Walter Pen-nel (rhymes with fennel)

HERITAGE
Hybridizer: Walter Pennell
Country of Origin: United Kingdom
Parentage: *C.* 'Vyvyan Pennell' x *C.* 'Daniel Deronda'

GROWING ZONES
USDA Growing Zones 4 thru 11.

BLOOMING PERIOD
Early in the season and repeats.

Height Range: Six to eight feet.
Light Exposure: It thrives equally in sunny
or shady locations.
Pruning: Optional or light.

HIGHLIGHTS
This clematis earns high marks for its exquisite coloring.
One of the prettiest clematis even in its single form.
A perfect choice for a tall obelisk.

ANECDOTAL
The renowned clematarian, Walter Pennell, named
this outstanding clematis after himself. During the
1950's, 60's and 70's, 26 new clematis hybrids
were attributed to Mr. Pennell.

C. 'Walter Pennell'

FLOWER FEATURES AND PLANT CHARACTERISTICS
The flower's tepals are painted a unique deep mauve-pink that
are streaked with a darker bar. In USDA Zones 4 thru 9 early
flowers are semi-double and fall flowers are single. In
USDA Zones 10 & 11 they are single only. The flower is
5" to 7" in diameter. Single flowers consist of 6 to 8 tepals.
Its stamens are a showy buff color.

Clematis 'Warsaw Nike'
(syn. *C.* 'Warszawska Nike', *C.* Midnight Showers)

{1982}

PRONUNCIATION
War-saw <u>Nee</u>-kay

HERITAGE
Hybridizer: Brother Stefan Franczak
Country of Origin: Poland
Parentage: Unknown

GROWING ZONES
USDA Growing Zones 4 thru 11.

BLOOMING PERIOD
Early in the season and repeats.

Height Range: Six to eight feet.
Light Exposure: It thrives equally in sunny
or shady locations.
Pruning: Optional or hard.

HIGHLIGHTS
Destined to be a classic because of its rich and seductive
coloring, this prolific bloomer's compact size makes it
a perfect container choice. Lovely when combined
with an apricot rose.

ANECDOTAL
Named after a memorial to Nike, the Greek goddess of victory,
which was erected in the city to commemorate the heroes of
Warsaw who fought for its freedom during World War II.

C. 'Warsaw Nike'

FLOWER FEATURES AND PLANT CHARACTERISTICS

The flower's tepals are dyed a rich velvety-purple. The flower
is 5" to 7" in diameter. Its stamens are yellow.

Clematis 'Westerplatte'

{circa 1994}

PRONUNCIATION
<u>Vess</u>-tur-plah-tuh

HERITAGE
Hybridizer: Brother Stefan Franczak
Country of Origin: Poland
Parentage: Unknown

GROWING ZONES
USDA Growing Zones 4 thru 11.

BLOOMING PERIOD
Early in the season and repeats.

Height Range: Up to six feet.
Light Exposure: It thrives equally in sunny
or shady locations.
Pruning: Optional or light.

HIGHLIGHTS
This clematis may have a difficult name to pronounce but it is
not difficult to appreciate its spectacular beauty. Blessed
with gorgeous coloring, its compact size makes it a
perfect container candidate.

ANECDOTAL
Westerplatte Peninsula at Gdañsk Bay is where the first shots
of World War II were fired. There is a monument there
commemorating the 182 heroic Polish soldiers who, for
seven days, defended the peninsula from the
Germans despite overwhelming odds.

C. 'Westerplatte'

Flower Features and Plant Characteristics
The flower's tepals are tinted a stunning deep velvety-red. The flower is 4" to 5" in diameter and has 6 to 8 tepals that are broad and overlapping. Its stamens are dark red.

Clematis 'Will Goodwin'

{1961}

PRONUNCIATION
<u>Good</u>-win

HERITAGE
Hybridizer: Walter Pennell
Country of Origin: United Kingdom
Parentage: Unknown

GROWING ZONES
USDA Growing Zones 4 thru 11.

BLOOMING PERIOD
Early in the season and repeats.

Height Range: Six to eight feet.
Light Exposure: It thrives equally in sunny
or shady locations.
Pruning: Optional or light.

HIGHLIGHTS
This clematis has beautifully formed tepals with
attractive frilled edges. It is a nice compact plant
that exhibits moderate growth. It is perfect to
grow in a container.

ANECDOTAL
William Goodwin was a long-time employee
of Mr. Pennell.

C. 'Will Goodwin'

FLOWER FEATURES AND PLANT CHARACTERISTICS
The flower's tepals are a very pretty pale lavender-blue. The
flower is 6" to 8" in diameter and has six to seven tepals.
Its stamens are yellow.

Clematis 'William Kennett'
(syn. *C.* 'William Kenneth')

{circa 1875}

PRONUNCIATION
William <u>Ken</u>-net

HERITAGE
Hybridizer: Henry Cobbet or George Jackman & Son
Country of Origin: United Kingdom
Parentage: *C. lanuginosa* x *C. patens*

GROWING ZONES
USDA Growing Zones 4 thru 11.

BLOOMING PERIOD
Early in the season and repeats.

Height Range: Six to eight (possibly ten) feet.
Light Exposure: It thrives equally in sunny
or shady locations.
Pruning: Optional or light.

HIGHLIGHTS
This venerable clematis is still very popular. It is prized
for being trouble free and for its prolific flowering ability.

ANECDOTAL
There is some debate among the clematis community about
who originally hybridized 'William Kennett'. Because
of ambiguities I found in my research,
I mention both possibilities.

C. 'William Kennett'

FLOWER FEATURES AND PLANT CHARACTERISTICS
The flower's tepals are colored a rich lavender-blue. The
flower is 7" to 8" in diameter and has 8 tepals
that are undulating and overlapping.
Its stamens are dark purple.

287

APPENDIX A
MUST-HAVE CLEMATIS
(BEST BETS FOR BEGINNERS)

'Duchess of Edinburgh'
'Ernest Markham'
'Marie Boisselot'
'Ramona'
'Rouge Cardinal'
'Star of India'
'Victoria'
'Ville de Lyon'
viticella 'Alba Luxurians'
viticella 'Etoile Violette'

APPENDIX B
10 CLEMATIS FAVORITES

'Aotearoa'
'Belle Nantaise'
crispa
'Daniel Deronda'
'Fairy Queen'
'Huldine'
'Proteus'
viticella 'Venosa Violacea'
'Walter Pennell'
'Warsaw Nike'

Appendix C
CLEMATIS BY COLOR
BLUE HUE
Important Note: There are *no* "true blue" clematis. They are periwinkle, lavender, purple or violet with a hint of blue shading on each tepal.

'Ascotiensis'
'Belle Nantaise'
'Blue Gem'
'Blue Light'
crispa
'General Sikorski'
'H. F. Young'
integrifolia
'Ken Donson'
'Lasurstern'
'Mrs. Cholmondeley'
'Mrs. P. B. Truax'
'Multi Blue'
'Perle d'Azur'
'Ramona'
'Sally Cadge' *(bicolor)*
'Sho-un'
viticella 'Blue Angel'
viticella 'Blue Belle'
'W. E. Gladstone'
'Will Goodwin'
'William Kennett'

Lavender/Lilac Hue

'Barbara Jackman' *(bicolor)*
'King Edward VII' *(bicolor)*
'Lady Northcliffe'
'Masquerade' *(bicolor)*
'Prince Charles'
'Victoria'
viticella 'Betty Corning'

Pink/Mauve Hue

'Asao' *(bicolor)*
'Bees Jubilee' *(bicolor)*
'C. W. Dowman' *(bicolor)*
'Carnaby' *(bicolor)*
'Charissima' *(bicolor)*
'Comtesse de Bouchaud'
'Dawn'
'Dorothy Tolver'
'Fairy Queen' *(bicolor)*
'Hagley Hybrid'
'Josephine'
'Lady Londesborough'
'Lincoln Star' *(bicolor)*
'Madame Baron-Veillard'
'Margaret Hunt'
'Mrs. Spencer Castle'
'Nelly Moser' *(bicolor)*
'Peveril Pearl' *(bicolor)*
'Piilu' *(bicolor)*
'Pink Champagne' *(bicolor)*
'Proteus'
'Scartho Gem' *(bicolor)*
'Sealand Gem' *(bicolor)*
'Sugar Candy' *(bicolor)*
texensis 'Duchess of Albany'

'Violet Elizabeth'
viticella 'Abundance'
viticella 'Margot Koster'
viticella 'Pagoda'
'Walter Pennell' *(bicolor)*

Purple Hue

'Aotearoa'
'Daniel Deronda'
x *durandii*
'Elsa Späth'
'Etoile de Malicorne' *(bicolor)*
'Gipsy Queen'
'Guiding Star'
'Honora'
'Jackmanii'
'Lady Betty Balfour'
'Lord Nevill'
'Perrin's Pride'
'Petit Faucon'
'Richard Pennell'
'Serenata'
'Star of India' *(bicolor)*
'The President'
viticella 'Emilia Plater'
viticella 'Etoile Violette'
viticella 'Mary Rose'
viticella 'Purpurea Plena Elegans'
viticella 'Venosa Violacea' *(bicolor)*

Red/Magenta Hue

'Barbara Dibley' *(bicolor)*
'Colette Deville'
'Ernest Markham'

'Niobe'
'Rouge Cardinal'
'Sunset'
texensis 'Gravetye Beauty'
texensis 'Sir Trevor Lawrence'
triternata 'Rubromarginata'
(bicolor)
'Ville de Lyon' *(bicolor)*
viticella 'Carmencita'
viticella 'Kermesina'
viticella 'Little Nell' *(bicolor)*
viticella 'Madame Julia Correvon'
viticella 'Minuet' *(bicolor)*
viticella 'Royal Velours'
viticella 'Södertälje'
'Voluceau'
'Warsaw Nike'
'Westerplatte'

CREAM/SILVER/WHITE HUE

'Belle of Woking'
'Duchess of Edinburgh'
'Gillian Blades'
'Henryi'
'Huldine'
'Jackmanii Alba'
'Lady Gray'
lanuginosa 'Candida'
'Louise Rowe'
'Marie Boisselot'
'Miss Bateman'
'Mrs. George Jackman'
'Otto Fröebel'
'Silver Moon'
'Snow Queen'
viticella 'Alba Luxurians'

YELLOW HUE

'Bill MacKenzie'
'Wada's Primrose'

APPENDIX D

BICOLOR CLEMATIS (CLEMATIS WITH A BAR)

'Asao'
'Barbara Dibley'
'Barbara Jackman'
'Bees Jubilee'
'C. W. Dowman'
'Carnaby'
'Charissima'
'Etoile de Malicorne'
'Fairy Queen'
'Lincoln Star'
'Mrs. N. Thompson'
'Nelly Moser'
'Peveril Pearl'
'Piilu'
'Pink Champagne'
'Sally Cadge'
'Scartho Gem'
'Sealand Gem'
'Star of India'
'Sugar Candy'
triternata 'Rubromarginata'
'Ville de Lyon'
viticella 'Little Nell'
viticella 'Minuet'
viticella 'Venosa Violacea'
'Walter Pennell'

DOUBLE CLEMATIS BY ZONES

Zones 10 & 11 (These clematis are doubles that do not require a winter chill or old wood.)
'Belle of Woking'
'Blue Light'
'Duchess of Edinburgh'
'Josephine'
'Multi Blue'
'Violet Elizabeth'
viticella 'Flora Plena'
viticella 'Purpurea Plena Elegans'

Zones 4 through 9 (Clematis listed below with an asterisk* require a winter chill and old wood to produce double flowers.)
'Belle of Woking'
'Blue Light'
'Daniel Deronda'*
'Duchess of Edinburgh'
'Josephine'
'Kathleen Dunford'*
'Louise Rowe'*
'Mrs. Spencer Castle'*
'Multi Blue'
'Piilu'*
'Proteus'*
'Violet Elizabeth'
viticella 'Mary Rose'
viticella 'Purpurea Plena Elegans'
'Walter Pennell'*

CLEMATIS FOR SUN ONLY

'Huldine'
'Lady Betty Balfour'
'Madame Baron-Veillard'
texensis 'Duchess of Albany'
texensis 'Gravetye Beauty'
texensis 'Sir Trevor Lawrence'
'Ville de Lyon'

SHADE CLEMATIS

'Asao'
'Barbara Dibley'
'Bees Jubilee'
'C. W. Dowman'
'Carnaby'
'Charissima'
'Dawn'
'Fairy Queen'
'Gillian Blades'
'Josephine'
''Lincoln Star'
'Louise Rowe'
'Nelly Moser'
'Otto Fröebel'
'Peveril Pearl'
'Pink Champagne'
'Proteus'
'Scartho Gem'
'Silver Moon'
'Wada's Primrose'

APPENDIX H
CLEMATIS FOR SHADE IN HOTTER LOCALES

'Barbara Dibley'
'Carnaby'
'Charissima'
'Gillian Blades'
'Josephine'
'Louise Rowe'
'Proteus'
'Scartho Gem'
'Silver Moon'
'Violet Elizabeth'

APPENDIX I
HEAT-TOLERANT CLEMATIS

'Aotearoa'
'Gipsy Queen'
'Jackmanii'
'Jackmanii Alba'
'Lady Betty Balfour'
'Serenata'
'Star of India'
'Victoria'
viticella 'Abundance'
viticella 'Alba Luxurians'
viticella 'Betty Corning'
viticella 'Blue Belle'
viticella 'Etoile Violette'
viticella 'Kermesina'
viticella 'Madame Julia Correvon'
viticella 'Royal Velours'
viticella 'Södertälje'
viticellla 'Venosa Violacea'

APPENDIX J
CLEMATIS FOR CONTAINERS

'Asao'
'Barbara Dibley'
'Barbara Jackman'
'Bees Jubilee'
'Belle of Woking'
'Blue Gem'
'Blue Light'
'C. W. Dowman'
'Carnaby'
'Charissima'
'Colette Deville'
'Comtesse de Bouchaud'
crispa
'Daniel Deronda'
'Dawn'
'Dorothy Tolver'
'Duchess of Edinburgh'
x *durandii*
'Elsa Späth'
'Ernest Markham'
'Etoile de Malicorne'
'Fairy Queen'
'General Sikorski'
'Gillian Blades'
'Guiding Star'
'H. F. Young'
'Hagley Hybrid'
'Henryi'
'Honora'
integrifolia
'Josephine'
'Kathleen Dunford'
'Ken Donson'

'King Edward VII'
'Lady Betty Balfour'
'Lady Londesborough'
'Lady Northcliffe'
lanuginosa 'Candida'
'Lasurstern'
'Lincoln Star'
'Lord Nevill'
'Louise Rowe'
'Marie Boisselot'
'Masquerade'
'Miss Bateman'
'Mrs. Cholmondeley'
'Mrs. George Jackman'
'Mrs. N. Thompson'
'Mrs. P. B. Truax'
'Mrs. Spencer Castle'
'Multi Blue'
'Nelly Moser'
'Niobe'
'Otto Fröebel'
'Perrin's Pride'
'Petit Faucon'
'Peveril Pearl'
'Piilu'
'Pink Champagne'
'Prince Charles'
'Proteus'
'Ramona'
'Richard Pennell'
'Rouge Cardinal'
'Sally Cadge'
'Scartho Gem'
'Sealand Gem'
'Sho-un'
'Silver Moon'
'Snow Queen'

'Sugar Candy'
'Sunset'
'The President'
'Ville de Lyon'
'Violet Elizabeth'
'Voluceau'
'W. E. Gladstone'
'Wada's Primrose'
'Walter Pennell"
'Warsaw Nike'
'Will Goodwin'
'William Kennett'

APPENDIX K

TALL CLEMATIS

'Aotearoa'
'Ascotiensis'
'Belle Nantaise'
'Bill MacKenzie'
'Gipsy Queen'
'Huldine'
'Jackmanii Alba'
'Jackmanii'
'Madame Baron-Veillard'
'Madame Grangé'
'Margaret Hunt'
'Perle d'Azur'
'Serenata'
'Star of India'
texensis
texensis 'Gravetye Beauty'
texensis 'Sir Trevor Lawrence'
triternata 'Rubromarginata'
'Victoria'

viticella 'Alba Luxurians'
viticella 'Betty Corning'
viticella 'Blue Belle'
viticella 'Emilia Plater'
viticella 'Etoile Violette'
viticella 'Kermesina'
viticella 'Madame Julia Correvon'

viticella 'Margot Koster'
viticella 'Royal Velours'
viticella 'Södertälje'
viticellla 'Venosa Violacea'

C. 'Ernest Markham'
& *C.* 'Henryi'.

ANATOMY OF A CLEMATIS

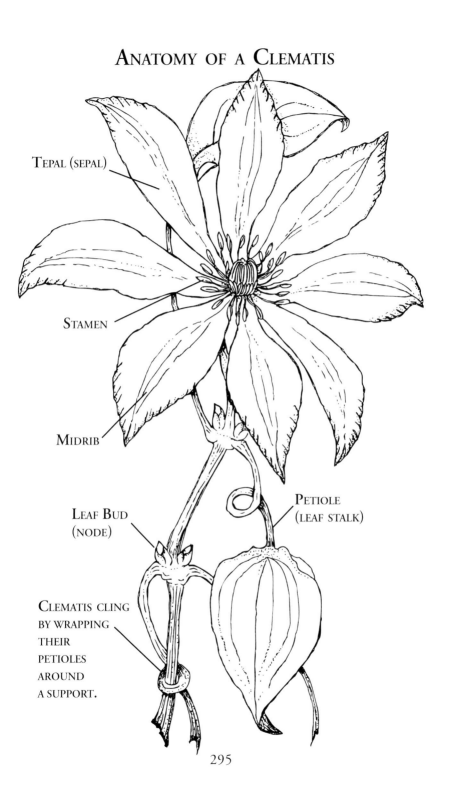

TEPAL (SEPAL)

STAMEN

MIDRIB

LEAF BUD
(NODE)

PETIOLE
(LEAF STALK)

CLEMATIS CLING
BY WRAPPING
THEIR
PETIOLES
AROUND
A SUPPORT.

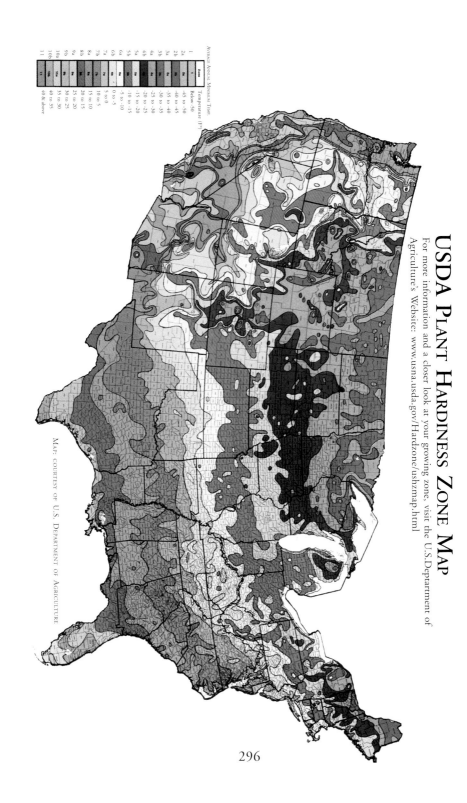

USDA Plant Hardiness Zone Map

For more information and a closer look at your growing zone, visit the U.S.Department of Agriculture's Website: www.usna.usda.gov/Hardzone/ushzmap.html

MAP: COURTESY OF U.S. DEPARTMENT OF AGRICULTURE

AVERAGE ANNUAL MINIMUM TEMP.

Zone	Temperature (F°)
1	Below -50
2a	-45 to -50
2b	-40 to -45
3a	-35 to -40
3b	-30 to -35
4a	-25 to -30
4b	-20 to -25
5a	-15 to -20
5b	-10 to -15
6a	-5 to -10
6b	0 to -5
7a	5 to 0
7b	10 to 5
8a	15 to 10
8b	20 to 15
9a	25 to 20
9b	30 to 25
10a	35 to 30
10b	40 to 35
11	40 & above

THE CLEMATIS GARDENER'S GLOSSARY

ACIDIC SOIL. Soil with a pH below 7.0.

ALKALINE SOIL. Soil with a pH above 7.0.

BAR. The central colored part of the tepal's midrib.

BICOLOR. A tepal having two colors.

Bud. The swelling on a stem that will produce leaf clusters and/or the part of the flower that produces a bloom.

CLEMATIS. The Greek word for some kind of climbing or trailing plant. The correct pronunciation is CLEM-uh-tis. Frequently mispronounced clem-MAT-is or clem-MATE-us.

CROWN. The portion of the plant where the stems join the roots and from which new shoots are produced.

CULTIVAR. A cultivated variety created by man to produce distinct and desirable characteristics. The names of cultivars are signified by single quotation marks and are always capitalized. For example, the cultivar 'Vyvyan Pennell' is a cultivated cross between 'Daniel Deronda' x 'Beauty of Worcester'.

DEADHEADING. The removal of spent or faded flowers to prevent seed production and encourage further flowering.

DECIDUOUS. Refers to a plant that loses its leaves at the end of the growing season. Although the majority of clematis are considered deciduous, they are unique in that the dead leaves most often remain on the plant.

DIEBACK. The rapid demise of a clematis starting at the tip of a stem. This condition can affect one stem or the entire plant. Dieback can be attributed to fungal disease, weather, lack of water, etc.

DISINFECTION. SEE SANITATION.

DORMANT (DORMANCY). The period in winter when a clematis temporarily stops growing. Dormancy for clematis may or may not occur in warmer locales.

DOUBLE FLOWERS. A clematis flower that produces multiple layers of tepals.

FUNGUS (PL., FUNGI). A lower form of plant life that includes molds, yeast and mushrooms. Fungi are the cause of most plant diseases.

HARDY PLANTS. Plants that are capable of enduring frost or freezing.

HERBACEOUS. A non-woody clematis which usually dies down to the ground at the end of the growing season. For example: *Clematis crispa* or *Clematis integrifolia*.

Horticultural disinfectant. A broad-range disinfectant that controls disease-spreading organisms.

Hybrid. A man-made crossbreeding of two different species denoted by an "x". For example: Clematis x 'durandii'. Clematis x durandii resulted from a cross between C. 'Jackmanii' x Clematis integrifolia.

Internode. The segment of the stem between nodes.

Leaf Bud. A bud that develops into a stem with leaves.

Midrib (flower). The central veins of the tepal.

Mulch. A layer of top dressing of organic material placed over the soil. Mulch enriches the soil, conserves water, reduces weeds and protects the roots from frost.

Node. The joint on a stem where a leaf or side shoot emerges.

Petiole. A leaf stalk. Clematis cling by wrapping their petioles around a support.

pH. A scale measuring the acid or alkaline content of your soil. 7.0 is neutral. Below 7.0 is acidic. Above 7.0 is alkaline. The ideal pH for clematis is 6.5.

Rootball. The mass of roots and soil that remains on a plant when it is removed from its container or dug out of the ground.

Rootbound. The condition that exits when a plant's roots outgrow the available space in its container. This situation can cause stunted growth and poor plant performance.

Sanitation. The process of eradicating fungal, bacterial or viral infection.

Sepal. See Tepal.

Single flower. A clematis flower with one layer of tepals.

Species. A distinct group of plants that share characteristics and interbreed freely.

Sport. New growth that spontaneously appears on a plant but bears no resemblance to the parent plant. Horticulturally it is an abrupt deviation or mutation. For example 'Multi Blue' (a double flower) is a sport of 'The President' (a single flower).

Stamen. The pollen-producing male part of a flower that consists of anthers and filaments.

Stem rot. A collapse, either totally or partially, of a clematis due to fungus.

Tepal. The colored petal-like segments that make up the outermost parts of the clematis flower.

Wilt. See Stem rot.

C. 'Ascotiensis' with *Rosa* 'Golden Celebration'.

INDEX

Bold page numbers indicate color pictures or illustrations.

CLEMATIS INDEX

C. viticella 'Södertälje' with a pink rose.

THE AMERICAN CLEMATIS SOCIETY

As you probably already know, clematis are an incredibly beautiful and versatile plant. The clematis I present in this book, though, are only the tip of the iceberg.

After reading *Simply Clematis* you will have noticed that the availability of certain varieties of clematis is limited. The misconceptions and misinformation that have surrounded clematis have contributed greatly to this lack of availability. It has certainly been an uphill battle we have waged against these invisible foes. Our society has, however, from its inception, been determined to win this battle and, through its efforts, I believe we will succeed.

However, there is still a lot of work to be done to make as many varieties of this wonderful genus available to the many gardeners out there who wish to enjoy them. This is why I would like to take the opportunity to invite everyone who reads this book to join our society.

The American Clematis Society is a non-profit organization whose sole purpose is to promote the understanding and proliferation of growing clematis in the United States. It is the first clematis society in the United States. Founded in 1996, it was originally named the Southern California Clematis Society but later evolved into the American Clematis Society. It is a society that is based on the premise that gardening should be fun and growing clematis should add to that enjoyment.

The dues are tax deductible and are used for publishing the quarterly journal, *The Clematis Chronicle*, as well as for postage, maintaining our website and other administrative expenses. For more information on the society and how to join please visit our website at www.clematis.org. Or, write to us at the American Clematis Society, P.O. Box 17085, Irvine, CA 92623-7085.

Clematis crispa